MILTON
a structural reading

For
Bebeann, Nickay, and Alessandra

MILTON

a structural reading

Donald F. Bouchard

Montreal

McGILL – QUEEN'S UNIVERSITY PRESS

1974

© Donald F. Bouchard 1974

First published 1974 by
Edward Arnold (Publishers) Ltd
25 Hill Street, London W1X 8LL

ISBN: 0-7735-0229-7

Library of Congress Catalog Card Number 74-82612
Legal Deposit 3rd Quarter 1974
Bibliothèque nationale du Québec

176954

Printed in Great Britain

Contents

Contents

Acknowledgements

Without a guide, it is difficult to enter Milton's labyrinth and the 'drear woods' of Milton criticism and it is next to impossible to find a way out, except with the model of the 'single just man'. No one works in isolation, and Milton scholarship supplies numerous examples of critical integrity, but those who have been especially helpful in my work have interests which are only indirectly related to Milton. Professors Sylvestor H. Bingham and Irving Massey have my gratitude, less for any particular contribution which they made to this book than for their example and faith in the processes of interpretation. Were it not for their accommodation to my 'failing ways', their generosity, and their compelling sense of intellectual rigour in our discipline, this book could not have been written.

More specifically, in terms of my interest and approach to Milton through the methods of French 'Structuralism', I wish to acknowledge my debt to Eugenio Donato and René Girard. Their friendship and contribution to my efforts cannot be measured and their influence is felt throughout this book. In addition, I thank my friends and colleagues at McGill: Mike Bristol, Chris Heppner, Peter Ohlin, Paul Piehler, Darko Suvin, Don Theall, and Ben Weems. They supplied advice and encouragement when it was needed.

The McGill Faculty Fund provided a grant which enabled me to complete the manuscript.

I

Introduction: *homo significans*

An unlearned reader, when he first opens his book, finds
himself surprised by a new language.
>   Samuel Johnson, *Lives of the English Poets*

The artist . . . recreates the course taken by meaning, he
need not designate it: his function, to return to Hegel's
example, is a *manteia*; like the ancient soothsayer, he *speaks*
the locus of meaning but does not name it.
>   Roland Barthes, 'The Structuralist Activity'

I

Milton supplies the example in *Paradise Lost*: every beginning
is 'in the middle'. Interpretation discloses the opposition of
inside and outside; not a gradual passage from the outside to
the inside, but a radical disjunction. From the point of view of
interpretation, to be outside is to be out of play and to dream a
natural progression beginning in a pure origin and 'founding
word'. In short, it is to envision the master-word of interpretation. This expectation is never realized, however, since interpretation is a contradictory activity. It may comfort itself with
the hope of a recuperative vision, yet, if it is to know itself, it
will be as a constant deferment of its goal. Interpretation moves
forward while maintaining its capability to recapture the past.
As a distinct activity, interpretation has an indefinite goal. If
interpretation is directed to discovering the *alpha* in the *omega*,
and if, for this reason, it presents itself with an obscure and
doubling goal, it is in order to perpetuate itself.

Interpretation is a labyrinth and is entered for something
other than itself; to a Theseus, who would battle the Minotaur
at the centre, the labyrinth is merely an obstruction, an unfortunate delay. It is penetrated for the best reasons, but once

the maze is entered, this motivation is obscured by the reason
of the labyrinth which needs no other. It is understood that
the labyrinth's reason is most visible at that point at which
Theseus finds himself lost because this is the time in which he
questions himself. The motivation which seemed sound on the
outside turns into doubt and the eternal certainties begin to
oscillate when the open and inviting avenues of the labyrinth
are discovered as dead ends. Something forces itself, is trying
to be said, in a labyrinth where what is hidden is an indirection
and a revelation. The double is hidden in the labyrinth and, in
due time, it will reveal Theseus as another double hidden in its
secret heart. The ways of the labyrinth are a self revelation.

This transformation is especially relevant to an analysis of
the Miltonic labyrinth. The 'darkness visible' of the first two
books of *Paradise Lost* hide and reveal the fallen space of
interpretation inhabited by Satan, the first model for critical
activity. His fall into the labyrinth of Hell represents his movement away from an uncritical acceptance of the Father's
plenitude: it is, as well, a movement 'in the middle', and a
precarious balance of extremes. His infinite descent contrasts
with his ascent to the throne of Hell; his blindness to his own
leadership in Hell contrasts with his judgement of the Father's
tyranny. These examples could be multiplied, but it is unnecessary: each of these equivocations points to the fact that Satan's
sight is directed outward. He sees the 'other' and is blind to
himself. As we learn in the soliloquy of Book IV, Satan can
escape Hell in his rejection and distancing of the 'other', yet,
he will never escape himself, because the double at the heart
of the labyrinth is the double heart of Satan. This meaning is
explicit when Satan encounters his progeny at the Gates of Hell
because Sin, we learn, is his long forgotten paramour. Satan
had obscured his true past and his love brings him back to his
origin in the creation of a 'sign portentous'.

At either end of the experience of Hell is a symbol of doubleness and the labyrinth is an artistic commentary and temporal
elaboration of this enclosed sign. On this level, the labyrinth
is the linear development of a writing which reveals and
obscures a forgotten conversation or it is culture, a self-
perpetuating mechanism which bars the door to the memory of
its origin. It is Thebes suffering the plague, but suffering more

pain at the messenger's arrival from Corinth. In other words, the labyrinth is destiny as script as Satan's experience in Hell is a living out of his unconscious past. The activity of Hell, of culture, and of interpretation is engaged in to guarantee that the past will remain buried. But, of course, the activity in Hell merely perpetuates the past as a present bondage in the sense that the script of the labyrinth is not an answer to an ancient question, but the question in contemporary disguise. Thus, Hell opens a double perspective of mystification and revelation and that the two are bound together in that revelation is intended to clarify the mysterious double light of Hell. Satan acts out his damnation in the confining spaces of Hell and his actions guarantee that his condition will persist. What appears as a way out for Satan is, in fact, a deeper movement into the heart of the labyrinth: the way out is the way in. Similarly, mystification is revelation of the 'other' at the centre of the labyrinth, where revelation discloses the self as mystified in its disclosure of the 'other'.

The labyrinth is a place of sacrifice: the Minotaur must be propitiated with the blood of the innocent. Satan justifies his sacrifice of the creation and of Adam and Eve through his undying hatred for the Father. He desecrates the creation because it is a sign of the Father's power. The implications of Satan's actions are even more interesting if we consider that the Garden of Eden, a symbol for a multitude of created beings, is constructed, both as a physical place and as representing the hierarchy of the animal kingdom, on the model of the pyramid. The Garden is a true pyramid, and, like the Egyptian pyramid which was both a tomb and a labyrinth. its function is to protect a sacred king. A pyramid signals the king's immortality and his continuing influence on human affairs. Moreover, the pyramid represents an elaboration of the principle of the labyrinth with its false doors and hidden passages. Satan is drawn to the Father's treasure house and is transformed into the intended victim, thus legitimizing the king's imposing majesty. The king lives on because of his power to exert revenge through the skill of his artifice. Satan wishes to dethrone the Father, but falls victim to his rationality exhibited in laws which live through time.

Labyrinths give the impression of haphazardness: they

appear to represent chaos and chance. To experience the
labyrinth, however, is to discover its meaning and the fact that
there is a law which governs its constitution. The law of chance
is based on series and repetitions and requires time to disclose a
statistical pattern. For this reason, the labyrinth is a temporal
elaboration. Wandering through the maze, certain junctures
are returned to in time or a dead end is reached which requires
a return and a new beginning. If it has a message, it counsels,
'Change your life', in forsaking the useless repetitions of the
maze. For what is encountered in the labyrinth is always the
same thing, although disguised as substitutions. Realizing this
is the revelation of the labyrinth's mystifications. With time,
then, comes clarification: the maze can be abstracted and its
purpose discovered. If revelation is the 'end' of form for Milton
('Form is the cause through which a thing is what it is'),[1] then
we can appreciate his intention to 'justify the ways of God to
men' in showing that justice is based on law, that God's ways
are intelligible, and that this law can be transcended in a new
life. Moreover, in this context, we can also examine the basis
of structure in *Paradise Lost* in terms of its 'lawful' repetitions.
As Roland Barthes has written:

> The syntax of the arts and of discourse is, as we know, ex-
> tremely varied; but what we discover in every work of
> structural enterprise is the submission to regular constraints
> whose formalism, improperly indicated, is much less im-
> portant than their stability; for what is happening, at this
> second stage of the simulacrum activity, is a kind of battle
> against chance; this is why the constraint of recurrence of the
> units has an almost demiurgic value: it is by the regular
> return of the units and of the associations of units that the
> work appears constructed, i.e., endowed with meaning;
> linguistics calls these rules of combination *forms*, and it would
> be advantageous to retain this rigorous sense of an overtaxed
> word: form, it has been said, is what keeps the contiguity of
> units from appearing as a pure effect of chance: the work of
> art is what man wrests from chance.[2]

[1] *The Works of John Milton* (New York: Columbia University Press, 1936),
XI, p. 59.
[2] 'The Structuralist Activity', *European Literary Theory and Practice*, ed.
Vernon W. Gras (New York: Dell Publishing Company, 1973), p. 161.

When discussing *Paradise Lost*, this description will be useful in determining Milton's technique of repetition, the manner in which his epic arises from chaos but is not chaotic. Equally, the whole range of Milton's work, it can be argued, foreshadows this prescription for structural activity.

II

Milton, an extremely self-conscious writer, supplies his own best interpretation: each of his works is both a decomposition and reconstruction of his productions from an earlier period. When developing an interpretation of Milton, it is necessary to keep in mind the structure of a given work, the repetitions which guarantee the intelligibility of 'forms'. In addition, Milton's repetitions, those which underlie and give stability to the many transformations in his long development, must be brought to the surface in any extended interpretation of his work. What, in short, remains constant in Milton's experience and expression? At this level, we discover that Milton's singularity cannot be reduced to personal idiosyncrasy. Milton, in his choice of forms and in his statements concerning a necessary 'tradition' in 'Of Education', saw his task as a continuation. It is one thing to argue that Milton broke with classical tradition by referring to Christ's denunciation in *Paradise Regained* or by pointing to his goal 'above th'*Aonian* Mount', but the simple fact remains that Milton could only surpass what he knew was given to begin with.

Yet, the debate continues. How do we come to terms with our conflicting judgements on Milton's self-conscious art; what of our critical repetitions? Our interpretations represent, and in this they differ little from the work of art, a decomposition and reconstruction of an earlier tradition: we, too, build a labyrinth and experience the confusion of Babel. At certain periods in the history of criticism, those times when critics are unsure of a shared community of interest, interpretation is nothing but polemic. The text is lost sight of as a critical opponent moves to centre stage. An earlier generation is questioned but history is ignored. The mediations of a given time and place are ignored, and, as long as this lasts, we can expect discomfirmations at the hands of a future generation. It is easy

to emphasize the misunderstandings of Dr Johnson and, more
recently, those of Eliot, concerning Milton, but is it recognized
that unless we emphasize our perspective from our own time
and place, we too will have failed in our enterprise? Nietzsche
argued that the 'general interest' of a scholar, his belief in the
pure and uncontaminated search for the truth, masked self-
interest and the polemical nature of interpretation. The critic
does not inhabit a 'universal mind', no more than anyone else,
nor is he without motivation. The critical stance is precisely a
standing *here* with its prejudices of place and its delimitation of
vision. For Nietzsche, this meant that one could not philoso-
phize about the nineteenth century without first recognizing
that it was a time of decay and weakness. Interestingly, according to Nietzsche, its most obvious sign of weakness was nothing
other than its need for philosophy.

Our situation has been succinctly stated by Jean Wahl:
'Nous sommes tous malades d'interpretation.'[3] The double
meaning needs emphasis: we are sick of and we are sick from
interpretation. A recognition of the role played by history in the
activity of interpretation would help to clarify our confusion.
The answer does not lie in a transcendence of history but in
recognizing the role history imposes on interpretation, specifically, in the critic's unconscious testing of himself against a
mutable and illusory reality. Mediation of a wayward history,
Milton shows, is not achieved by opposing an earlier generation,
by setting present novelties against those of the past, or by
adding counter-accusation to earlier accusations. Rather, in
a Miltonic context, the only legitimate response to history is a
questioning and overcoming of the self insofar as this self
employs interpretation to gain recognition. As Jacques Lacan
maintains, the goal of literature and criticism, of any thoughtful
activity, is to transform the 'desire for recognition' into a
'recognition of desire'.[4] For Milton, it is to become a rational
being aware of his roots in the irrational; not the irrational as
unintelligible, but as compulsive and repetitive behaviour.
Realizing this, it is possible to foster through interpretation a

[3] Cited by Eugenio Donato in 'The Two Languages of Criticism', *The
Languages of Criticism and the Sciences of Man*, eds. Richard Macksey and
Eugenio Donato (Baltimore: The Johns Hopkins Press, 1970), p. 97.
[4] 'The Insistence of the Letter in the Unconscious', *YFS*, 36–7 (1966),
p. 143.

rational community much as Milton felt in *Areopagitica*, that free publication and open discussion had the effect of creating a brotherhood bound by the unifying spirit of truth. Milton's 'fountain of truth' is ubiquitous; no one is given the final word except to point to the underlying reason for discussion and debate: the erection of a new temple of free inquiry. This is a healing vision only insofar as it points to interpretation as an on-going, communal enterprise where truth is the product of relationship, and where truth has no substantive or a priori status.

Censorship is, of course, opposed to this understanding, yet a far more indirect and subtle alternative to interpretation in Milton's time was given by the Royal Society. To simplify the issue, it can be said that the members of the Royal Society were joined in the common pursuit to repair the loss of Adam, specifically, the loss of Adam's ability to name things properly, a loss further aggravated in the building of Babel. The programme of the Royal Society was nothing less than purification; purging language of its false associations and re-naming things with mathematical precision. It should be apparent that this enterprise comes close to the moral imperatives of censorship and that, in practice, the desire for purification can be used to justify a 'reign of terror'. This is partially speculative, yet the conclusion seems credible if we can agree that a language devoid of ambiguity and double meaning is not a key to the 'new found land' unless utopia is a state of willing regimentation supported by a unidimensional language flowing from an elitist 'House of Solomon'. In our day, the battle lines are drawn between semiology and hermeneutics, nevertheless, the issue is the same.

The end of interpretation, it is understood, could be achieved through the common acceptance of a system of classification. But is it also recognized that this entails moving outside history? This possibility was, in fact, envisioned by Milton and explains his preoccupation with Ramus logic and his writing of the *Art of Logic* and the *De Doctrina Christiana*, the other side of the millennial aspirations found in *Comus* and 'Lycidas'. With the apocalypse, history would be self-consumed, leaving the 'saints' to rebuild the kingdom of the spirit. History, however, did not disappear; rather, the idea of a kingdom was the first casualty

of the prose warfare. The failure of the puritan idea, at least
in its 'pure' form, may have been experienced as a loss by
Milton, but it also lead to his reconsideration of this phase of
his career in *Paradise Lost*. Indeed, not a total loss, merely, the
loss of an external paradise and a subsequent cultivation
of the 'Paradise within'. Milton's prose was more than an
interlude, because without it, *Paradise Lost* would probably
have remained unwritten. Instead, he would have produced
a providential history and a vindication, with,

> long and tedious havoc (of) fabl'd Knights
> In Battles feign'd; the better fortitude
> Of Patience and Heroic Martyrdom
> Unsung;
>
> (IX, 30–33)

The 'better fortitude' of *Paradise Lost* represents Milton's
overcoming of his private plans and public history, and, for
this reason, Milton's epic is an act of courage and intelligence.
As René Girard has recently said:

> I am personally convinced that truly great works of art,
> literature, and thought stem, like Oedipus' own reinterpreta-
> tion of the past, from a genius' ability to undertake and
> carry out a radically destructive reinterpretation of his
> former intellectual and spiritual structures. Unlike lesser
> works, perhaps, these masterpieces will pass the test of the
> most radical structural interpretation because they partake
> of the same essence, to a higher degree, no doubt, than our
> most searching analyses.[5]

An inhabitant of a physical and spiritual darkness, the narrator
and scribe of *Paradise Lost*, like Moses, carries the burden of the
law and this action excludes him from the promised land. The
meaning of his actions is always more than he can say, yet, his
actions are meaningful in the organization of the text. He bears
witness to the truth in his uneasy passage through the epic, a
truth always before him and, because of this, partially incomprehensible. The reader, however, as one who witnesses the
narrator's plight, can experience the encompassing structure

[5] 'Tiresias and the Critic', *The Languages of Criticism*, p. 20.

of the text and can appreciate the manner in which *Paradise Lost* is a 'radically destructive reinterpretation' of Milton's former works.

III

Interpretation is a labyrinth directed to the disclosure of the double, and, taking our lead from Milton's activity in *Paradise Lost*, this book is directed to following the labyrinthine course of the double through the chronology of Milton's work. Milton's history sets the direction and it would take a different book to show the manner in which his development relates to the radical changes which were taking place in his time. Milton's work, in other words, needs to read side by side with Michel Foucault's *Les Mots et les Choses*, the records of the Royal Society, the seventeenth-century exegetical work on the Bible, and the political and religious history of the Revolution. Yet, Milton's output has consistency and can be examined in its own right as an internal and integral development, which assumes his sensitivitiy to the changes taking place in his time. Milton's development is dialectical and, for this reason, this book is divided into three sections: the first section deals with a selected group of works before *Paradise Lost*; the second is exclusively an analysis of *Paradise Lost*; and the third deals with *Samson Agonistes* and with *Paradise Regained*, works which develop the double strands of the argument pursued in *Paradise Lost*.

For Milton, an examination of the double centres on its relationship to idolatry. The ethical considerations of this preoccupation are obvious, but what is less so is the way in which idolatry is the basis of an iconic and mimetic art. Thus, the three stages of Milton's career are discussed in terms of a prelapsarian and fallen aesthetic as they correspond to a mimetic and interpretative art, or in terms of mystification and revelation. In this context, it is argued that in *Comus* and, to a lesser degree, in 'Lycidas' and the prose, Milton supports his desire for community through artistic mystifications. The labyrinth of history is overcome through divine intercession where communal and apocalyptic myths guarantee the ascendancy of the righteous. In the prose, as early as *Areopagitica*, however, Milton discovered that history does not favour any

single group, that it is nothing other than the perpetual oscillation of good and evil. In other words, history is the double
which had been exorcised in *Comus* in the apparition of Sabrina.
History is the debate between the Lady's two brothers and an
extension of their contending interpretations. As Milton found
in the prose, each of his tracts required a subsequent defence.
If the prose has a single lesson, it is that interpretation in history
is endless and circular: 'The king is dead, long live the king.'

The darkness of the prose is illuminated in *Paradise Lost* by
concentrating on the nature of the sign. This entails an examination of language as it derives from the creation of the 'image'
in Christ, the first action in Heaven and the one which determines the course of the text as either a Satanic adventure or as
a recreative act. Again, *Paradise Lost*, a labyrinthine text,
opens onto a double way in the mystifications of Satan and the
repetitions and oscillations of history and in the revelation of
the sign, through the example of Christ, as the end of interpretation. The latter alternative counsels the end of a 'last
judgement', which represents the end of history and the col-
lapse of the labyrinth.

With *Paradise Regained* and *Samson Agonistes*, we find Milton's
continuing preoccupation with interpretation and the manner
in which this activity conditions a particular technique, and,
in these works, the distinctions between an innocent and fallen
aesthetic are related to the forms of drama and epic. The miracle
which concludes the actions of Samson balances the plain
intentions of *Paradise Regained*; plain words versus miraculous
intervention. In this reading, the play is presented first—the
dating of these two works remains debatable—because the
words of *Paradise Regained* are posited in terms of a sensual
banquet and the seemingly miraculous dispensations in the
catharsis of drama. Moreover, the two relate as Old to New
Testament with the saving words of *Paradise Regained* a response
to the ambiguity of words which evolve from the Old Testament
sense of the singularity of a 'chosen people'. Put differently,
Samson Agonistes is a literary product and *Paradise Regained* its
interpretation. Christ's purpose in the short epic is to come to
terms with a miracle similar to that which ends Samson's
career. A further reason for this juxtaposition is to question the
traditional separation of literature from criticism as two

distinct activities. Their similarity is more impressive than their differences in that both are decompositions and compositions of a sign which gives meaning to the labyrinth of interpretation.

PART I
'In order serviceable'

2

'Sacred vehemence': the limits of opposition

Idolatry consists in making, worshipping, or trusting in idols, whether considered as representatives of true God or of a false one.

Milton, *On Christian Doctrine*

When one is young, one venerates and despises without that art of nuances which constitutes the best gain of life, and it is only fair that one has to pay dearly for having assaulted men and things in this manner with Yes or No. Everything is arranged so that the worst of tastes, the taste for the unconditional, should be cruelly fooled and abused until a man learns to put a little art into his feelings and rather to risk trying even what is artificial—as the real artists of life do.

Nietzsche, *Beyond Good and Evil*

The uncompromising attitudes of youth need a mask to hide all that is inhuman and cruel in the excesses of idealism and in this respect Milton was little different from any of us. The mask which came ready to hand for him was that of community in the utopian ideal of *Comus*.[1] It is the end toward which all the action of the masque is directed: to lead the Bridgewater children back to their parents at the end of the pageant having been tried in the 'drear woods' of illusion, the opposite of fruitful community. Or so it seems, even though Milton's depiction of the joys of community is not altogether one-sided,

[1] Gale Carrithers, 'Milton's Ludlow *Mask*: From Chaos to Community', *Critical Essays on Milton from ELH* (Baltimore: The Johns Hopkins Press, 1969), pp. 103–22.

since we learn early in the masque that Comus's desire for the
Lady is conditioned by the fact that her song recalls memories
of his childhood home:

> I have oft heard
> My mother Circe with the Sirens three,
> Amidst the flowery-kirtled Naiades,
> Culling their potent herbs and baleful drugs,
> Who, as they sung, would take the prisoned soul,
> And lap it in Elysium: Scylla wept,
> And chid her barking waves into attention,
> And fell Charybdis murmured soft applause.
> Yet they in pleasing slumber lulled the sense,
> And in sweet madness robbed it of itself;
> But such a sacred and home-felt delight,
> Such sober certainty of waking bliss,
> I never heard till now.
>
> (251–64)

We are reminded of Satan's speech in Book Four of *Paradise
Lost* when he first sees Adam and Eve; they also remind him
of home and of his degeneration since his rebellion. Although
Comus learns to adapt to the 'hospitable woods' (187), he
desires to return to a common home, something like the 'All in
All' of *Paradise Lost*. The difference between Comus and the
Lady, however, is that for him, home is a past condition, where
for her it lies ahead, a promise if she can extract herself from
the 'woods' of deception and isolation.

The effects of home, however, remain evident in the Lady
as Comus realizes overhearing her song: it is a promise and
potentiality always at her disposal in a nature which has been
instilled with virtue. But this concept of home requires purification in a stripping away of the associations made by Comus
as a refuge from the work of salvation. For among the effects
of Comus's spell is metamorphosis:

> Soon as the Potion works, their human count'nance,
> Th' express resemblance of the gods, is chang'd
> Into some brutish form of Wolf, or Bear,
> Or Ounce, or Tiger, Hog, or bearded Goat,

All other parts remaining as they were.
And they, so perfect is their misery,
Not once perceive their foul disfigurement,
But boast themselves more comely than before,
And all their friends and native home forget,
To roll with pleasure in a sensual sty.

(68–77)

Nevertheless, home is a constant and underlies all the various transformations: it is the 'genius' of the place as symbolized by Sabrina as, more generally, it stands for the virtuous (however mythical) genealogy of England where home takes on the encompassing aspect of the 'Chosen Seed'. So that built into the Lady's response to Comus is a utopian aspiration conveyed by the pastoral context:

Impostor, do not charge most innocent nature,
As if she would her children should be riotous
With her abundance; she, good cateress,
Means her provision only to the good
That live according to her sober laws
And holy dictate of spare Temperance:
If every just man that now pines with want
Had but a moderate and beseeming share
Of that which lewdly-pamper'd Luxury
Now heaps upon some few with vast excess,
Nature's full blessings would be well dispens't
In unsuperfluous even proportion,
And she no whit encumber'd with her store,

(762–74)

In an earlier context, the pastoral intention is even more apparent when the Lady mistakes Comus in his disguise:

Shepherd, I take thy word,
And trust thy honest offer'd courtesy,
Which oft is sooner found in lowly sheds
With smoky rafters, than in tap'stry Halls
And Courts of Princes, where it first was nam'd,
And yet is most pretended:

(322–7)

Opposed to this utopian ideal, a theme amplified by the Attendant Spirit through his reference to his 'mansion' as the 'Garden
of the Hesperides' in the Epilogue, is the 'rout of Monsters'
which follows Comus. They comprise a group described in the
stage direction preceding Comus's first speech as entering
'making a riotous and unruly noise', and, in this respect, they
are antithetical to a state founded on 'unsuperfluous even
proportion'. Again, the theory is more than simply an append-
age to the dramatic development of the masque, for implicit
in the Lady's judgement is her capacity as singer. In the
language of *Paradise Lost* the Lady feeds,

> on thoughts, that voluntary move
> Harmonious numbers; as the wakeful Bird
> Sings darkling, and in shadiest Covert hid
> Tunes her nocturnal Note.
>
> (III, 37–40)

Not only is she the reason for the masque, but she supplies its
motive power. Eventually, her song will bring all the participants together in the final dance of celebration as the 'light
fantastic round' of Comus is transformed into the Lady's
'harmonious numbers'.

The final effect, although little different from that achieved
by the Jonsonian masque, for instance, as a festive celebration
of James I, does accomplish something quite unexpected in its
handling of the pastoral scene. In the pastoral, as in the pastoral
drama, what is being recorded is the seasonal and cyclical
aspect of nature; emblematic of this in the masque are the
dance and a festival commemorating the completion of a cycle,
a correspondence intended as thanksgiving for the abundance
of nature. As C. L. Barber has shown with respect to Shakespeare's handling of this pastoral moment, it represents, as
well, the overturning of hierarchies and ordinary categories
and expectations.[2] This explains the nature of the last dance
in *Comus*: breaking down the theatrical illusion, spectators join
the masquers in the dance and the action is led by the 'Country-
Dancers'.

In this perspective, the aristocratic values of the brothers and

[2] *Shakespeare's Festive Comedy* (Princeton: Princeton University Press, 1959).

the Lady are meant to be ineffectual against the blandishments
of Comus and the confusion of the 'drear woods', since their
response to the abundance of nature is largely negative.
Rather than getting to the 'root' of things, they resort to
idealism, egotism, and, after all is said, to a false show of
heroic courage, as underlined by the Attendant Spirit:

> Alas good vent'rous youth,
> I love thy courage yet and bold Emprise,
> But here thy sword can do thee little stead;
>
> (609-11)

The philosophy of the brothers, like that of their sister, is
intended for defence and not celebration; it is a protective
armour against forces from outside. But it not only locks out,
it also locks in, blinding the youths to all but their sense of
urgency and terror. A similar doubleness in the use of protective
devices is found in Milton's handling of the angels' armour in
the 'War of Heaven'. Such is the effect of a philosophy of
opposition, of taking too literally the puritan metaphor of
warfaring Christian. The Elder Brother's 'all or nothing'
philosophy is potentially tragic, for if virtue is assailed and
hurt, 'surprised by unjust force' (590) and 'enthralled' as it is
by Comus, then 'The pillar'd firmament is rott'nness / And
earth's base built on stubble' (598-9).[3]

Throughout the masque, the youths would convince us of
the credibility of their perceptions, that their perceptions are
sufficiently encompassing to withstand any temptation or
aggression. The Elder Brother's equation of the world and its
fate with his own private fears and perception of persons and
events is seriously questioned in the most obvious way, in that
he is uninformed, in contradistinction to the audience, as to
the supernatural origin of the masquers who participate in the
action; for this reason, his words are often unintentionally
ironic. We need to be as cautious of the pronouncements of the
Lady and her brothers as we are of the hero's statements in
Samson Agonistes, because in both contexts we encounter characters who are in varying degrees self-blinded.

The youths, lost in woods similar to Spenser's 'wood of

[3] Carrithers, 'Milton's Ludlow *Mask*', p. 111.

Error' in the *Faerie Queene*, enact their condition much as Samson does as captive of the Philistines. They, like Samson, read their plight as one extending to the world's 'various objects of delight'. We encounter the Lady, a misanthrope early in years:

> This way the noise was, if mine ear be true,
> My best guide now; methought it was the sound
> Of Riot and ill-manag'd Merriment,
> Such as the jocund Flute or gamesome Pipe
> Stirs up among the loose unletter'd Hinds,
> When for their teeming Flocks and granges full
> In wanton dance they praise the bounteous *Pan*,
> And thank the gods amiss.
>
> (170–77)

The woods have enchanted her senses, transforming order into 'wanton dance'. We know, of course, that the woods are neither good nor bad, just as the two shepherds encountered in the woods do not necessarily stand for a single condition. The shepherd can be either Comus or the Attendant Spirit. This ambiguity has its comic side, since it reminds one of the underlying assumptions of comedy, as represented by the sub-title of Shakespeare's *Twelfth Night*, 'What You Will'. As Malvolio shows, the characters in comedy ordinarily find what they are looking for, even though in acting out their desires, they ultimately are undercut by the 'realistic' demands of the genre. In any event, the Lady expecting 'riot and ill-manag'd Merriment', is not disappointed as she encounters Comus and his 'rout of Monsters'.

Her desires, of course, are never kept hidden from the audience:

> A thousand fantasies
> Begin to throng into my memory,
> Of calling shapes and beck'ning shadows dire,
> And airy tongues that syllable *men's names*
> Of Sands and Shores and desert Wildernesses.
>
> (205–9, my italics

She is aware of this tendency and brings to her aid the memory of earlier instruction: faith, hope, and chastity—the last, a disturbing substitution for many critics, but understandable, certainly, in terms of her education and the plight confronting her. Her brothers, mirroring her plight, and in this sense transforming her narcissus song into an indication of the action to follow, are quick to seize on the sexual nature of her venture into the 'leavy labyrinth', particularly, Second Brother insistent on 'Savage hunger . . . Savage heat' (358) and the 'ill-greeting touch' which promise to fulfil the Lady's fantasy. In answer to this desire, Elder Brother offers inaction and the belief that the power of chastity can 'freeze her foes to congeal'd stone'. Exactly the opposite situation holds when they find the virgin in Comus's palace. How then are we to understand the transition from this condition, one brought on partly as an effect of her 'fantasy', to the charity which knits all together at the end of the masque?

The dramatic quality of the masque cannot be ignored, and neither can a context of illusion which gives rise to difficulties. But, more specifically, what gives rise to problems in *Comus* is absence, an absence which creates the need for finding the Lady who has wandered off from her brothers who, themselves, had earlier left her in search of refreshment to quench her thirst. (She finds refreshment and comes to lament her 'thirst'—the desire which created her plight.) Beyond this, is the condition of the woods which signifies the absence of light, a condition also abetted by the absence of moon and stars, as the Elder Brother remarks:

> Unmuffle ye faint stars, and thou fair Moon
> That wont'st to love the traveller's benison,
> Stoop thy pale visage through an amber cloud,
> And disinherit *Chaos*, that reigns here
> In double night of darkness and of shades;
>
> (331-5)

The absence of natural signs is interpreted as chaotic and this leads, in turn, to a 'double night', representative of a general condition of doubleness where words are separated from things, the source of the masque's ambiguity. It is this situation which creates a condition where Comus can read nature's abundance in an exactly opposite way from the Lady, and it is this discontinuity between natural fact and language which informs the discussion of the brothers. Dealing with Elder Brother's first set of speeches, Gale Carrithers has written:

> . . . he quickly betrays a speculative and quasi-philosophical egotism which disables him for dealing with the world around him. Brooks and Hardy rightly emphasize both the possibility and the unawareness on his part that the real world may not 'square with the ideal one which he has constructed for himself'. . . . In the speech beginning with the sober practicality of 'Peace brother, be not overexquisite' (359) he quickly launches into elevations, circumlocutions, slippery equivalences, quasi-philosophical verbosities as if words were magic enough without community association.[4]

In a world experienced as devoid of meaning, a meaning only possible through the aid of the gods who control nature, the brothers would play god in forcing their own meaning on things. In their speeches, they dwell on the passive aids of contemplation and chastity, but invariably this softness is a mask for violence:

> Do ye believe me yet, or shall I call
> Antiquity from the old Schools of *Greece*
> To testify the arms of Chastity?
> Hence had the huntress *Dian* her dread bow,
> Fair silver-shafted Queen for ever chaste,
>
> (438–42)

And further, in a context which engages Elder Brother more directly:

> . . . I'll find him out,
> And force him to restore his purchase back,
> Or drag him by the curls to a foul death,
> Curs'd as his life.
>
> (606–9)

---

[4] Carrithers, 'Milton's Ludlow *Mask*', pp. 106–7.

As we know, Elder Brother is held back by Thyrsis, since Thyrsis is aware that violence against Comus would be useless: 'he with his bare wand can unthread thy joints / And crumble all thy sinews' (613–14). The Attendant Spirit informs the brothers that against Comus more subtle means must be taken; opposed to heroic behavior will be the device of a 'certain Shepherd Lad / Of small regard to see to, yet well skill'd / In every virtuous plant and healing herb' (619–21). The usual interpretation of this opposition would be to see it as pride versus humility with the ultimate ascendancy belonging to the unprepossessing 'shepherd lad'. But what is at stake here is the good medicine of the shepherd, as opposed to that of the brothers, against the contagion of Comus. Specifically, the battle is not between the brothers and the shepherd, but between Comus's 'orient liquor' and the shepherd's 'small unsightly root'.

Poison and antidote cancel each other out, and the Lady is left in her chair, 'in stony fetters fixt and motionless'. This represents both the limits of the brothers' philosophizing, since the bulk of their argument is to prove that their sister will remain unmoved (stony) to Comus's medicine, and the stasis to which she has given rise in her initial fantasies and the thoughts she brings to mind to combat her sexual longings. It is no longer a question of the good victorious over the bad, as the brothers would have us believe, but of the indifference of good and evil.

The moral gloss aside, Comus is suggesting an idyllic bacchanal in honour of 'great Pan', while the Lady wishes to maintain her superiority and difference. What sustains her is the myth of chastity, of *Dian* or *Minerva*, 'unconquer'd Virgin / Wherewith she freez'd her foes to congeal'd stone, / (With) rigid looks of Chaste austerity / And noble grace that dash't brute violence / With sudden adoration and blank awe' (448–52). The Lady's identification with the gods reveals not only that her condition is the result of a 'brute violence' directed against her, like that sustained by *Dian* and *Minerva*, but that the only way to combat violence is through a reciprocal violence. In addition, a further interpretation seems called for which accounts for the engendering of the gods themselves, in that their status as gods depends on a new and more powerful violence than that which opposes them. The Greek Pantheon does little else than stage the endless warfare of the new and old gods, and individual human destiny, in this context, is based on a certain arbitrariness: 'when any favor'd of high *Jove*' (78). To be either good or evil, virtuous or impious depends on being 'favor'd of high *Jove*' as well as the side chosen in the war of the gods.

The particular mythic antagonism found in Comus is between Dionysus and Orpheus: Dionysus, according to Euripides in *The Bacchae*, being the god of crowds, of the 'rout of Monsters' in *Comus*, while Orpheus, a new god, is identified as the harmonizer of misrule and undisciplined crowds.

In *Comus*, all the details associated with the cult of the older god, Dionysus, are either represented as philosophical errors (the 'drear woods', for that matter, are his realm) or as illusion. Orpheus, on the other hand, represents light and truth and, as importantly, he is the basis upon which true community can be founded. The Lady, strongly identified with Orpheus in her ability as singer which creates 'Divine enchanting ravishment' (245), constantly returns to her desire for a new, more equitable, and lasting community based on 'even proportion' and is opposed to Comus's older cult attached to natural rhythms and to her own natural desire for the Dionysian as illustrated by her 'fancy'. For nature in the masque stands for enslavement to a degenerate form, best illustrated in the narcissus theme. Losing oneself in nature as Narcissus did, is to be 'perfect in (one's) misery' (73) and to fall into self-deception: '(they) not once perceive their foul disfigurement, / But boast themselves more comely than before' (74–5).

In the crisis generated by the conflict of Dionysus and Orpheus, the sacred, that is, the source of legitimate rule and the basis of virtue which allows the construction of a new cult and community, is being contested and its nature examined. Nothing is settled and everything is possible in the opening between the old and the new. Attempting to control the potentialities of this open space, men would be gods in each other's eyes, but, as we have seen, what this means in practical terms is polemic, the form of dialogue which comprises the bulk of *Comus*, and violence, although this violence is partly obscured by the polemics. For the sacred is violent in its origin insofar as men in their impiety fail to acknowledge the new gods.

In Milton's own version of this mythic origin we find
Sabrina:

> Whilom she was the daughter of *Locrine*,
> That has the Scepter from his father *Brute*.
> She, guiltless damsel, flying the mad pursuit
> Of her enraged stepdam *Guendolen*,
> Commended her fair innocence to the flood
> That stay'd her flight with his cross-flowing course.
>
> (827–31)

In time, Sabrina is vindicated, as time 'with his cross-flowing
course' is the arena in which Milton's values, like those of the
Lady which are expressed by the Attendant Spirits as resulting
from 'due steps' (12), will come to supplant the mystifications
of pagan rites. The impulse of time, the Christian and messianic
reading of time, is purification:

> So dear to Heav'n is Saintly chastity,
> That when a soul is found sincerely so,
> A thousand liveried Angels lackey her,
> Driving far off each thing of sin and guilt,
> And in clear dream and solemn vision
> Tell her of things that no gross ear can hear,
> Till oft converse with heav'nly habitants
> Begin to cast a beam on th'outward shape,
> The polluted temple of the mind,
> And turns it by degrees to the soul's essence,
> Till all be made immortal
>
> (453–63)

And in an even more explicit passage:

> Yea even that which mischief meant most harm
> Shall in the happy trial prove most glory.
> But evil on itself shall back recoil,
> And mix no more with goodness, when at last
> Gather'd like scum, and settl'd to itself,
> It shall be in eternal restless change
> Self-fed and self-consum'd;
>
> (591–7)

That Sabrina is vindicated in the historical myth of England is indicative that 'evil on itself shall back recoil'. This belief seems particularly dear to Milton, as we find him rehearsing an alternate form of this idea some ten years later in a famous passage from *Areopagitica*:

> He that can apprehend and consider vice with all her baits and seeming pleasure, and yet abstain, and yet distinguish, and yet prefer that which is truly better, he is the true warfaring Christian. I cannot praise a fugitive and cloistered virtue, unexercised and unbreathed, that never sallies out and sees her adversary, but slinks out of the race where that immortal garland is to be run for, not without dust and heat. Assuredly we bring not innocence into the world, we bring impurity much rather: that which purifies us is trial, and trial is by what is contrary. That virtue therefore which is but a youngling in the contemplation of evil, and knows not the utmost that vice promises to her followers, and rejects it is but a blank virtue, not a pure; her whiteness is but an excremental whiteness; which was the reason why our sage and serious poet Spenser, whom I dare be known to think a better teacher than Scotus or Aquinas, describing true temperance under the person of Guyon, brings him in with his palmer through the cave of Mammon and the bower of earthly bliss, that he might see and know, and yet abstain.[5]

The passage is often quoted and for good reason, for it seems to summarize the distinctive attitude which Milton took to his own art as a didactic instrument which stages a trial by contraries, and its application to *Comus* and the education of the youths is obvious, if only the initial stance of the Lady is interpreted as a potential example of 'excremental whiteness'.

The happy ending of the masque is to a certain degree the product of a successful trial, but, equally, it is the logical consequence of a national history exemplified by a succession of 'true warfaring Christians'. Thus, the ending is the product

---

[5] *John Milton: Complete Poems and Major Prose*, ed. Merritt Y. Hughes (New York: Odyssey Press, 1957), p. 728. Unless otherwise indicated, all future references are taken from this text.

of millennial aspirations which conceive of England as a utopian community.

The youths have been rescued by a myth, a myth illustrated by the story of Sabrina which gives it a nationalistic flavour, while, at the same time, emphasizing, as Sears Jayne has argued,[6] its source in the humanist Neo-platonic currents of the day, and, as with all myths, its function is to point to the fundamental difference of good and evil. Yet, the masque is also the product of poetic de-mystification to the extent that it stages a polemic encounter between good and evil, where, in the language of *Areopagitica*, the 'two twins cleaving together'[7] are often difficult to distinguish in the violence generated by their encounter, and to the extent that Milton amplifies the masque form, ordinarily given over to spectacle and amusement, to include the rendering and imitation of a crisis both personal and cultural.[8] The ambience of *Comus* is the result of a Fall where 'the knowledge of good is so involved and interwoven with the knowledge of evil, and in so many cunning resemblances hardly to be discerned'. That good and evil can finally be separated and 'discerned' is largely due to the extra-textual identification of the Lady with Sabrina, of the super-imposition of a redemptive mythology onto the actuality of a night-time journey through the woods of error. In addition, the happy ending depends on the nature of truth as a repressive instrument, its ability to drive 'far off each thing of sin and guilt'. Even then, however, the matter is far from clear in that truth, identified in Neo-platonic terms with light, enters a world of darkness, represented by the labyrinth of the woods, and introduces not light but an in-between state of shade, and it is the ambiguity of this middle state, similar to that depicted by the Neo-platonists in their conception of the soul's descent into the world, which we find in *Comus*.

In order to achieve regeneration, the soul has need to sacrifice a part of itself, what early in the masque we found expressed in terms of the Lady's imaginings and fancy and in Younger

---

[6] 'The Subject of Milton's Ludlow *Mask*', *Milton: Modern Essays in Criticism*, ed. Arthur Barker (New York: Oxford University Press, 1965), pp. 88–91.

[7] Hughes, p. 728.

[8] Carrithers speculates that a 'costly battle' underlies the equivocations of the masque (p. 105).

Brother's emphasis on 'savage heat'. More generally, what is
sacrificed is the world, and, more particularly, the natural world
with its meaningless repetitions and its perplexing cycles; for
the circle is substituted the straight line of redemption. This
can only be seen from a distance, the specific distance represented by the Attendant Spirit who descends from the Hesperian
field to help the youths, for while caught up in their experience,
the youths read their journey as a meandering in a woody maze
where they endlessly repeat their faltering steps without beginning and end.

The youths, as we know, must give up the natural world,
at least that nature represented by Comus, but, as importantly,
they must give up their pretensions to divinity, a divinity which
assures them control over the dark underworld of Comus,
because the maze is the product of the interweaving of the
natural and the divine. Divinity and all human claims to
divinity are expelled at the end of the masque and the human
participants, like the audience, emerge from the baffling context of 'sacred vehemence' to the encapsulating reassurance of
the Spirit's epilogue. As the Spirit came from 'Regions mild
of calm and serene Air' (4), so the epilogue records his return
to 'those happy climes' (977). The intention is clear: it is the
gods who have been sacrificed and expelled from the action,
so that the youths can be introduced into the human community purged of vainglory and impiety, not to mention the
Dionysiac passions which the gods exhibit. While the youths
are caught between the warring gods, a war which, incidentally,
is being fought over territorial imperatives as described in the
prologue, they are, in effect, in the power of their wrath,
because their war implies, in practical terms, personal revenge.
In another context, the Lady recognizes this aspect of the conflict: 'That he, the Supreme good, t' whom all things ill / Are
but as slavish officers of vengeance . . .' (217-18).

The Dionysian current which runs through the masque and
which contaminates the action in terms of conflict, unruly
noise, and meaningless repetitions is an expression of wrath
caused by the youths' failure to recognize the power and bene-
ficence of 'great Pan'. Once this power is acknowledged as one
extending to the benign influence of the river Severn from
which Sabrina arises, the wrath of the gods is ended and the

Lady is able to stand, indicating that she personally resolved
the contending polarities of Dionysus and Orpheus. As well,
this recognition entails the knowledge that the youths' experi-
encing of nature as a state of illusion is due to their participation
in the divine: the illusion, in short, followed from the belief in
the 'unblemish't form of Chastity' as a human dispensation
which could place the Lady on the level of the gods. The
subordination, however, of man to the gods is real and must be
accepted before order is restored. Only with this acceptance
can the state described in the epilogue be fulfilled:

> But far above in spangled sheen
> Celestial *Cupid* her fam'd son advanc't,
> Holds his dear *Psyche* sweet entranc't
> After her wand'ring labors long,
> Till free consent the gods among
> Make her his eternal Bride,
> And from her fair unspotted side
> Two blissful twins are to be born,
> Youth and Joy; so *Jove* hath sworn.
>
> (1003–11)

We might wonder at the reputed 'free consent' of the gods
after having viewed an application of their method of dialogue
in the masque as based on disagreement, conflict, and sophistic
argument. But, it is important to differentiate: this is the side
of the gods exemplified by Comus, a god in his involvement in
the world, and the effect of the masque is to create a distance
between the gods and man so that the twins of contrariness and
opposition can be transformed into 'blissful twins', representative of charity and civic responsibility. Thus, in terms of its
best conception, *Comus* calls for the endless work of regeneration
in a human community dedicated to love where the changes to
be effected are primarily internal in the development of virtue.
This implies, as well, that the attitude of the youths, all too
ready to lay the blame for their imperfections on someone else,
is not particularly attractive, since the changes they desire are
essentially external; they operate on the assumption that if the
world were changed there would be no problems and, for this

reason, are ever in need of discovering scapegoats—someone 'out-there' who hampers their good intentions. But so long as they seek solution to their difficulties outside themselves, they will remain lost in the 'woody maze'.

3
The 'dread voice' and 'dearest pledge': beyond oppositions

As he moves forward within his environment, Man takes with him all the positions that he has occupied in the past, and all those that he will occupy in the future. He is everywhere at the same time, a crowd which, in the act of moving forward, yet recapitulates at every instant every step that it has ever taken in the past. For we live in several worlds, each more true than the one within it, and each false in relation to that within which it is itself enveloped. Some of these worlds may be apprehended in action, others exist because we have them in our thoughts: but the apparent contradictoriness of their co-existence is resolved by the fact that we are constrained to accord meaning to those worlds which are nearer to us, and to refuse it to those more distant. Truth lies rather in the progressive expansion of meaning: but an expansion conducted inwards from without and pushed home to explosion-point.

Lévi-Strauss, *Tristes Tropiques*

(i) Uncouth swain

Potentially, the 'drear wood' of *Comus* signifies the end of significance and coherence in the world, since it stands for a condition where, in the main, good is indistinguishable from evil and where words are equivocal. What makes the woods a labyrinth is precisely the fact that human passion has transformed words into ambiguous counters in the search for truth, a transformation abetted by Comus's art as an instrument of doubleness. Language now has a double reference: the object referred to and the moral state of a subject who voices his identifications. Thus, we find that both Comus and the Attendant Spirit are initially identified as shepherds, and, also, that the ravishment produced by the Lady's song is similar to that of Comus's 'mother *Circe* and the Sirens three' (253). Equally, we find that the verbal encounter of Elder Brother's optimism with the younger one's pessimism can only achieve a philosophic stalemate, and that even with the instruction of Thyrsis, they are unable to liberate their sister from Comus's art and magic. The objective of the masque, however, is to purge itself of the ambiguities created by a subjective reading of things so as to achieve at the end 'unsuperfluous even proportion'', and the way in which this is done is by purifying the intentions of the youths.

As importantly, however, from the artist's point of view, this purification requires a realization that at the source of his difficulties is the nature of art as an instrument aligned with the beautiful, understood in terms of symmetry, which can lead to a condition where the artist, narcissus-like, seeks his own reflection in his work. The artist creates something beautiful and opposes it to the bestial and distorted (beauty and the beast) in the hope that his creation and example will lead to reformation.[1] But to achieve this end, he deals in illusion and opens himself to the charge that he, and no one else, is responsible for having set loose the beast which feeds on beauty, thus placing himself in a fundamentally ambiguous position. In terms of this arrangement, it is the poet who can be charged with the loss of coherence. The situation becomes far more interesting when the artist inserts himself in his own creation, as we find Milton doing in 'Lycidas'.

It is not so much a question of Milton's identity to the 'uncouth Swain', an alias intended to represent Milton's sincere grief at the death of a close friend, as his staging the poetic function confronting the loss of coherence in the death of a young and promising poet like himself. As many critics have realized, 'Lycidas' is far more than the lament of one friend for another, for it represents the poet meditating on his craft,

---

[1] This matter has been dealt with in detail by Professor Peter Ohlin in an unpublished essay, 'King Kong and the Mechanical Bride'.

and, particularly, meditating on its apparent uselessness in a
world of action.

What is being tested, in addition, is the poet's belief in his
own difference, the fact that he is set apart as an example of
virtue, and that, by his calling, he is meant to set the pattern
of regeneration. What profoundly disturbs the 'uncouth Swain',
in this respect, is that death threatens to not only destroy this
ambition, but the very difference which sustains him. For
what characterizes death is its arbitrariness and, specifically,
its failure to respect the poet's difference. This, in any case,
seems to be the conception, which Milton develops in 'Lycidas'.

In an earlier context, in 'Elegy VI', Milton's conception of
death is antithetical to his version in 'Lycidas'. In the earlier
poem, death is introduced only to show its powerless nature
when confronting the rule of virtue:

> So Homer, the spare eater and the water-drinker, carried
> Ulysses through vast stretches of ocean, through the monster-
> making palace of the daughter of Phoebus and Perseis,
> through the seas made treacherous by the songs of the Sirens,
> and through your mansions, O infernal King, where he is
> said to have constrained the hosts of shades by means of a
> libation of dark blood. For truly, the bard is sacred to the
> gods and is their priest. His hidden heart and his lips alike
> breathe out Jove.[2]

It is merely a game meant to enhance the power of the poet.
What saves Homer, as a model for all poets, is the 'golden
mean': 'spare eater and water-drinker'. In this respect, Homer
is opposed to 'monster-making palace', to 'the songs of the
Sirens', 'the seas made treacherous', and so forth, and this benevolent capability is the product of inspiration in 'his hidden
heart and lips (which) alike breathe out Jove'. But the problem
arises: how is the poet to distinguish true inspiration from that
which informs the demonic Siren's song?

Comus has shown that to be involved in the contest of good and
evil, even though the poet invariably maintains his righteousness, is, in actuality, to be caught up in a situation of reciprocity where good and evil are indiscernible as 'two twins

[2] Hughes, p. 52.

cleaving together'. The force of the debate in *Comus* is to contaminate both sides of the argument, especially as we see the
opposing camps attempting to sustain their virtue, their difference, in terms of a degenerate other. But this difference, as the
violence of the opposition becomes increasingly evident, that
is to say, the non-difference of the positions, as both become,
from an objective point of view, equally vindictive, or as both
are seen with increasing clarity as being 'out for blood', is
always upheld by subjectivity in the creation and acting out of
myths, dreams, and fantasies. As was argued in the reading of
Comus, the resolution of the masque comes about through the
introduction of a millennial dream, since only in this way can the
youths be rescued from the ambiguity created in the con-
frontation of good and evil. Moreover, the fantasy cuts through
the entire masque, affecting and contaminating both the
individual characterizations and the redemptive structure which
is developed in the action. The ending is, in actuality, no different from the beginning: everything is settled beforehand,
and for this reason, it is unlikely that the audience would be
disturbed by the presentation, for they are invited to read into
the ambiguous action of the masque the myth of virtue and
chastity.

In other words, *Comus* represents the coming of age of the
brothers and their sister, but as certainly, it represents the
coming of age of the audience's fantasy, which is legitimized in
the myth of Sabrina and by their millennial expectations.
Milton's masque is, indeed, a 'Siren' song for the gathering at
Ludlow Castle, especially if the audience misinterprets the
events as a hymn to Jove. As 'Siren song', however, it is no
doubt successful, in that it allows the audience and participants
to ignore their origin as a mixed state of good and evil in a
dark wood of deception.

Seen differently, it can be argued that Sabrina's magic is
stronger than the incantations of Comus because she can transform him into a scapegoat, yet, as importantly, her magic serves
to obfuscate his expulsion, the specific fact that the youths'
regeneration requires the metamorphosis of Comus into a
scapegoat. It's as if nothing had happened: another 'mid-
summer night's dream'. Perhaps, this is also the case because
the Lady offers a constant centre to the interest of the audience,

and one which also affects the reader, since her conduct represents the inhibitions and obfuscations of the myth she enacts. She puts into practice a myth which is only legitimized at the end of the masque, and it is in this sense that the myth can be said to contaminate the action, since from the beginning, the Lady stands for an essential difference (faith, hope, and chastity) which is the product of the myth's final repression of the passions. Indeed, she is 'frozen at the centre'—an abstract superimposed onto what would otherwise be a dynamic interchange. The real encounter of the masque is not between the Lady and Comus but is to be found in the debate of the brothers, a debate replete with hopes, fantasies, and text-book learning as content to prop up a lame subjectivity. This, too, is forgotten in the resolution.

When we turn to 'Lycidas', then, we find this ambiguity resurrected, only this time the 'uncouth Swain' is directly engaged in a first person encounter with the arbitrariness of death: 'Comes the blind *Fury* with th'abhorred shears / And slits the thin-spun life' (75–6). Faced with this condition, with what seems a life made meaningless by death, the speaker oscillates between hope and despair—a sign of his natural affinity for the pagan idea of fortune. This individual response to a cyclical pattern is developed in terms of context in 'Lycidas'. Happiness is to be unaffected by death; such it was to be 'nurst on self-same hill' (23). A world of serenity, peace, and endless time: 'and both together heard / What time the Gray-fly winds her sultry horn' (27–8). It is to be seemingly outside of nature and in control, a state like that represented by the blue sky of *Comus*, free of the heat and care of this 'pinfold'. Despair follows from a movement into a space 'confined and pester'd' where men 'strive to keep up a frail and feverish being'. As the spatial model of the wheel of fortune makes clear, the contradictory feelings of sad / happy, hope / despair correspond to the spatial orientation of up / down, in / out. In 'Lycidas', this distinction and correspondence is at the heart of the poem's emotional force: Cambridge, where Milton and King were students together under the tutelage of 'old *Damaetas*', versus the site of the shipwreck near the mouth of the river Dee and the mythical burial place of Welsh bards. Separating the two spots are not only contrary outlooks, but two different worlds,

the crucial difference of life and death. This geographical
opposition used to underline particular emotional responses
is not new in Milton. It is the basis, for that matter, of *L'Allegro*
and *Il Penseroso*, and later, in *Paradise Lost*, the device will be
used again in the spatial characterizations of Heaven and
Hell.

What is being sought, however, in 'Lycidas' is a context
which will unite these opposites, and the formulation, at first,
seems paradoxical: 'sunk low, but mounted high' (172). This
should not necessarily strike us as problematic, for the poem
is precisely concerned with the understanding of obstacles,
the most obvious of which are to be found in paradoxes and,
most obviously, in the moral paradox that the good die young.

Nature and death, as a natural phenomenon, present themselves at first as the most tangible obstacles to the speaker's
'consolation', but these difficulties stem from something more
fundamental: the speaker's own unreadiness and scepticism.
As the poem progresses, we learn that the most pressing and
disturbing stumbling-block to conviction and 'saving' faith
is a speaker whose words and behaviour argue against the
apostolic mission of Christ. The problem of interpretation is
largely solved once we realize that the speaker has inadvertently
supplied the key to his puzzlement, or, more exactly, 'two
massy Keys', where 'the Golden opes, the Iron shuts amain'.
For, as the St Peter passage develops, we learn that the keys
relate to the call of the church which is represented as a bounti-
ful gift but one which is constantly being appropriated by 'such
as for their bellies' sake / Creep and intrude and climb into
the fold' (114–15).

Returning to the beginning of the poem, it is possible to see
that the conventional pastoral opening has a deeper meaning in
terms of these keys. Under the guise of pastoral, the 'uncouth
Swain' is being called to a ministry and, also, to a banquet.
Death, seen as a stumbling-block in the way of an earlier
pastoral contentment, is, on the contrary, an invitation to a
greater and more lasting pleasure, 'the blest Kingdoms meek
of joy and love' (177). Once the welcome and call is acknowledged, all the obstacles fall away and nature itself is revivified.
Thus, death, as the major barrier to faith, is also the only opening onto faith; it is at once a closure and an opening.

A similar recognition occurs in George Herbert's poetry; from the point of view of 'closure', faith is 'The Collar', and oppositely, it is 'one calling', the caller. Faith, then, is an invitation, a vocation, a special calling, and only through faith can one enter into the 'fold'; any other way, and 'the Iron shuts amain'. In 'Lycidas', the opposition of the keys is explicitly defined in terms of a 'calling':

> Of other care they little reck'ning make,
> Than how to scramble at the shearers' feast,
> And shove away the worthy bidden guest;
>
> (116–18)

The call comes at a low point, in keeping with the logic of 'sunk low, but mounted high':

> Alas! What bouts it with uncessant care
> To tend the homely slighted Shepherd's trade,
> And strictly meditate the thankless Muse? ...
>
> *Phoebus* repli'd, and touch'd my trembling ears
>
> (64–77)

Unexpected, but more importantly, given as it is out of context, the call goes unanswered because unrecognized in the pastoral idiom. And the frantic search for an answer continues: one begun in the hope of 'lucky words' is picked up again in the invocation to 'smooth-sliding *Mincius*; crowned with vocal reeds' (86). The message would seem to be that there is no answer to the questions being posed, and the lack of response leads to a general indictment:

> It was that fatal and perfidious Bark
> Built in th' eclipse, and rigg'd with curses dark,
> That sunk so low that sacred head of thine.
>
> (100–102)

This is a desperate resolution. What consolation can follow this statement? Looking for an answer, searching for someone or something responsible for the loss, a loss which is later interpreted as 'foul contagion' (127), the speaker settles, Oedipus-like, on a general impiety, the result of a fallen human nature. From the vantage of pastoral, the speaker remains secure in his claims of righteousness. Such is the hidden message of the Orpheus section: the responsible party is that 'rout that made the hideous roar' (61). In identifying with Orpheus, the 'uncouth Swain' is purged of guilt, but at the price of being ineffectual. He may be comforted, but what of his duty to Lycidas?

Nevertheless, he persists in setting himself apart, as a 'perfect witness of all-judging *Jove*' (82). The reference in this line is to fame, not simply an indiscriminate fame, however, but the speaker's, who will prove himself in the demanding form of the pastoral elegy.[3] Unequal to the task, he will fall upon the idea of original sin as a last resort at justification, bringing with it another obstacle, that of the 'dread voice'. Not a call or an opening, not a welcome to a new life; rather, a finality in an apocalyptic judgement:

> But that two-handed engine at the door
> Stands ready to smite once, and smite no more.
>
> (130–31)

(ii) 'The false heart'

In the most immediate and understandable sense, the prophetic intensity of judgement in 'Lycidas' underscores its moral basis. As John Skinner's book on the prophet Jeremiah shows, a difficulty is encountered once the distinction is sought between the justified prophecy of the one who hears the 'voice of Yahwe' and that of the false prophet. The fact that a prophet centres his teaching on doom and retribution is no guarantee of his sacred inspiration, since it is claimed by good and false alike. According to Skinner, Jeremiah devises a far more practical method in distinguishing the true prophet:

The real test which Jeremiah applies to his opponents is the test of *morality*. It is not so much in the form of their prophetic

---

[3] Donald Friedman, 'Lycidas: The Swain's Paideia', *MS*, III (1971), p. 3. Professor Friedman describes the poem as enacting the 'psychological pattern of resistance and acceptance'.

experience as in the substance of their prophetic teaching
that he discovers the proof that they are no true spokesmen
of Yahwe. In their indifference to the sin of the people, in
their positive encouragement of evil-doers, and in their
immoral lives, they proclaim their entire ignorance of
Yahwe's truth. It is the men themselves who are false; and
to the false heart no true revelation is vouchsafed. Hence he
knows that they are no accredited messengers of the God
whose essence is righteousness, that the visions by which they
seek to authenticate their message cannot come from Him
and must therefore be in some way the product of their own
minds.[4]

Thus the call in the St Peter passage is for moral reformation as
an end in itself, yet, equally, as an indication of having heard
the voice of God, the only justification for righteous inspiration.
A moral life justifies the teacher's claim to inspiration in being
the only verifiable response to the call of faith. Morality is the
way into the fold; any other method is but to 'creep and intrude
and climb into the fold' for one's own sake and not as the result
of true inspiration.[5] This interpretation of morality as a sign of
true inspiration, or, in Luther's terminology, as a sign of vocation, is a commonplace of Protestant thought,[6] and it also
poses difficulties, for we are still faced with the ambiguity of an
open way which is closed as men attempt to expropriate this
truth for their own use. More directly, in terms of 'Lycidas',
Wayne Shumaker points out in reference to the second 'digres-
sion': 'St Peter next appears as the "Pilot of the *Galilean* lake",
the description providing an ironic contrast to the reader's
knowledge that King was *not* rescued from the sea.'[7]

As Milton insists in 'On the Morning of Christ's Nativity', the
oracles are 'mute'. They continue to trade on the miraculous,

[4] *Prophecy and Religion* (Cambridge: Cambridge University Press, 1961),
p. 195.
[5] *Cf.* Hughes, p. 830. In the autobiographical insertions of the *Second
Defense*, Milton emphasizes his desire to serve as an example of moral
reformation.
[6] For the Reformation idea of vocation and its bearing on Milton's early
career, see Michael Fixler, *Milton and the Kingdoms of God* (Evanston:
Northwestern University Press, 1964), pp. 46–75.
[7] 'Flowerets and Sounding Seas', *Milton: Modern Judgments*, ed. Alan
Rudrum (London: Macmillan, 1968), p. 99.

but, as Skinner argues in his interpretation of Jeremiah, this
is a matter of form without substance:

> The hungry sheep look up, and are not fed,
> But swoln with wind, and the rank mist they draw,
> Rot inwardly, and foul contagion spread;

                                                    (125-7)

Again, the 'Pilot of the *Galilean* lake' does not possess the key;
what he holds is two keys. In terms of the intent of the poem,
consolation and rejuvenation, the St Peter passage respresents
an application of the second key which 'Shuts amain' while,
indirectly, it reveals the nature of the other key. In other
words, not only is the pastoral to be read as a dark statement of
the Christian light and truth, but, conversely, the doom of the
St Peter passage must itself be understood for the hope it offers.

The doubleness of image and response as part of the poem's
intention underscores the contradictory pagan and Christian
views of nature as fatalistic and redemptive, and, similarly,
(this is too often forgotten in a reading of 'Lycidas') it points
to the fact that scripture is open to interpretation and can be
read as a source of dissension and as the 'fountain' of truth
which unifies. In the spirit of Augustine's *De Doctrina Christiana*,
Milton was to write some years later in *Areopagitica*: 'How many
other things might be tolerated in peace and left to conscience,
had we but charity, and were it not the chief stronghold of our
hypocrisy to be ever judging one another.'[8]

If the Bible is a form of divine 'accommodation' for Milton,
it is, nevertheless, an 'accommodation' which can serve the
ends of both good and evil. The Bible, as a social document, as
a historical record of the divine truth put into practice, is of
concern for Milton not as a static and unmovable truth, but in
the way in which it can clarify and ease the burden of human
relationships. For this reason, judgement is the foremost
obstacle to truth, in the sense in which the New Testament
truth centres on the closure of judgement as a dispensation to
mankind. Since at the heart of judgement is the desire for
justification, the act of judgement is idolatrous—the love of self
and of one's own judgement at the expense of others.

[8] Hughes, p. 747.

Therefore, from the human perspective of the 'uncouth Swain', judgement reveals doubleness: the Fates and Atropos, the 'two-headed engine'. Moreover, this doubleness forms the poet's understanding of Lycidas, himself, as the representative of dead virtue, and more specifically, of the double standard where the good die young.

Again, the speaker would avoid the recognition of the doubleness created by judgement as he attempts to re-establish his sacramental function in the flower sequence. But, draping the hearse of the dead shepherd, he is struck by the uselessness of his task:

> For so to interpose a little ease,
> Let our frail thoughts dally with false surmise.
> Ay me!
>
> (152-4)

There is no consolation in this single and unproblematic task, 'Whilst thee the shores and sounding Seas / Wash far away . . .' (154-5). The 'dread voice' remains present as it continues to contaminate the pastoral intention, transforming the melancholy plaint of the flower section into a description of the 'monstrous world', at the 'bottom' of the desire for retribution and judgement. Wrath produces more wrath, as judgement calls for a counter-judgement, until it is satisfied. It will not be appeased by the sacrificial flowers, 'like to that sanguine flower inscrib'd with woe'. Rather, it calls for human blood, 'my dearest pledge'. In this sense the 'gory visage' of Orpheus prefigures the 'dearest pledge' of Christ, and it is this context which sets the pattern for Lycidas.[9]

We begin to understand the issue being raised in 'Lycidas', when we fasten onto the problem of imitation underlined by a typological reading of the poem and found in the various prefigurations which lead to the acceptance of King into 'the blest Kingdoms meek of joy and love'. For, what is given at the beginning of the poem is a virtuous shepherd who has learned to imitate the proper behaviour of the shepherd's calling. He learns his lesson well, 'and old *Damaetas* lov'd to hear our song'.

---

[9] *Cf.* Kathleen M. Swain, 'Retributive Justice in "Lycidas": "The Two-Handed Engine" ', *MS*, II (1970), pp. 119-29.

After this acceptance, he is struck dumb by what appears to be a radical rejection: 'but O the heavy change'. Attempting to make sense of this radical alteration of his state (it is this search which creates obstacles), he searches for scapegoats—something or someone responsible for the loss. As long as the search is directed outside himself, the answers are inconclusive and misleading. For, what blinds the speaker is this very search for justification, thus, the oscillation from heroic valour to despair. The search in response to the stumbling-block represented by the radical rejection of the shepherd continues to uncover obstacles. This is the 'Fall', the heavy sentence which occurs in the 'eclipse', since it stands for the endless repetition of a search doomed to failure and since the impetus for the search is the result of the blinding caused by the obstacles.

All too easily the desire to 'somewhat loudly sweep the string' is transformed into questioning, longing, and despair. In locating a scapegoat, the speaker unfortunately finds himself, or, what amounts to the same thing, his alter-ego, Lycidas, as witness to a fallen world. How, then, will he find consolation and the answer which will dissolve the duality of the speaker's intentions?

The irony is that Lycidas is invited to the 'shearer's feast', but as the sacrificial offering, and in this lies the golden key. As René Girard observes in his discussion of the prophetic understanding of the scapegoat figure, what distinguishes the Christian from the pagan sacrifice is that Christ was a willing sacrifice.[10] This, in Miltonic terms, is the measure of Christ's liberty: to know and yet to suffer all. Enacting a paradox like that of 'sunk low but mounted high', Christ sacrifices himself in order to put an end to sacrifice and all its surrogates: idolatry, self-love, pride, and the warfare and judging which fosters 'tyranny and superstition'.

Like Christ, the narrator at the beginning of the poem insists that he is unprepared to undergo his Gethsemane. Having learned by its ending, however, that the death of the self is necessary to faith,[11] he can touch the very nature of his plight and the source of his earlier irresolution: 'Weep no more, woe-

[10] 'Symétrie et Dissymétrie dans le Mythe d'Oedipe', *Critique*, February 1968, p. 109.
[11] Friedman, 'Lycidas', p. 18.

ful Shepherds weep no more, / For *Lycidas* your sorrow is not dead' (165–6). Lycidas is dead; not his sorrow. Christ's passion lives on as the completion of the pattern which must be imitated, the willing sacrifice which ends discord and the assertions of self. Death, rather than defeating the pastoral intention, becomes the means of achieving and intensifying the pastoral desire for equality in a utopian community where scapegoats are unnecessary, since the call goes out to willing victims, 'meek in joy and love'.

(iii) Repetitions

'Lycidas' and *Comus* are radically different poems. The differences range from the most superficial to the profound. *Comus* is smooth and, for all its highlighted argumentation, is uneventful, while 'Lycidas' is all roughness and indecision. In the former, the certainties and answers are given early in the piece and are, for the most part, authenticated by the poem's happy ending. As good is shown victorious over evil, the myth of chastity is vindicated. The masque becomes problematical only when the function of myth is questioned, that is to say, when myths are shown to be instruments of reciprocal repression which produce scapegoats whose expulsion has the happy effect of allowing one to forget that such a device was ever needed. Having been involved in a rivalry, graphically expressed in the masque by 'this marble venom'd seat / Smear'd with gums of glutinous heat' (916–17), the ending allows an opportunity of escaping from the conflict with 'chaste palms moist and cold' (918). Our hands are clean, as the myth not only vindicates the audience, but allows the Lady the luxury of misunderstanding or forgetting (it comes to the same thing) the hazard of the woods. A critical reading of the poem, consequently, is critical to precisely the extent that it is suspicious and disenchanted with this mechanism. Beginning with this feeling, the writer will be led to uncover the source of his discontent in the undertow of myth. Either we have a masque as didactic instrument, pandering to the desires of an audience who, themselves, are the product of the myth being illustrated, an act of self-indulgence, or *Comus* is a true poem which, in staging a myth, discloses its arbitrariness.

In most readings of the masque, Comus is treated badly, and, of course, this can be justified, since he appears throughout as a true demonic agent. What we need to realize, however, is that Comus is evil because he represents a contamination—not bad 'in essence', but as the result of a mythic context. The poem was written with the ending in mind, with the realization that Comus posed no real threat, since he would be expelled at the end, and it is this fact which transforms him from a potentially festive and recreative character into a type of Satan. Whatever dramatic interest the masque develops, therefore, depends on our realization of this mechanism, and the further realization that the real issue of the masque is to be found in the bravado, pessimism, anger, and hopelessness of the two brothers. For it is the brothers who enact the rivalry implicit in the myth. The obvious fact is that were it not for the self-absorption of the brothers, the Lady might not have become lost (one of them could have stayed with her while the other searched for 'some cool friendly Spring' (282), and there would have been no performance. The Lady is safe and will remain secure through all time; the brothers, on the other hand, are unresolved and remain so even with the help of Thyrsis. In *Paradise Lost*, it is the brothers who will reappear in the central rivalry of Satan and Christ, and the Lady will be transformed into the snare of beauty which she represented, however indirectly, in *Comus*.[12]

When we turn to 'Lycidas', the situation is reversed: the problems are on the surface and the saving mechanism is un-recognized although always implicit in the pastoral context. For in 'Lycidas' the myth no longer functions. No longer a saving truth, it becomes an instrument of doom, an accusation which returns to haunt the speaker. Orpheus is dead and could not quell 'the rout that made the hideous roar'. Searching for a way out, for a culprit, a scapegoat, to take the blame, the speaker discovers himself as victim, as the one chosen for sacrifice. The crisis recreated in 'Lycidas' records the de-mystification of the myth, in the recognition that myths had always called for human blood. What underlies the catharsis of *Comus* is the destruction of the 'other's' value system. This the 'dread voice' exemplifies, and, in terms of the speaker's

[12] Another instance of 'Beauty and the Beast', the warfare of Christ and Satan representing the beastliness of recrimination.

unconscious response, it leads us to the awareness that to sustain
the self at the expense of the other is always to be off balance,
oscillating between joy and despair. It is this recognition
which leads to the logic of the willing sacrifice and to a stance
beyond the momentary gratifications of myth. In this respect,
there is little difference between Christian and pagan myths,
because both can be used to encourage idolatry and superstition.
The pattern set by Christ, however, whose 'sorrow is not dead',
is to reinterpret redemptive myths as a call to self-sacrifice. This,
in fact, is the 'dearest pledge' of 'Lycidas'.

Where in *Comus* the issue of idolatry is obscured by the propensity of the brothers and the Lady to transform chastity
into an idol, and where we are all too ready to accept this
transformation under the pretext of Christian truth, in 'Lycidas'
this pretext is at the centre of the speaker's preoccupation with
obstacles, of the closed versus the open way. In addition, it is
necessary to grasp the nature of the 'call' as iconoclastic in the
destruction of obstacles in seeing that they represent a false
problem and misunderstanding.

Repetition is the key to the obstacle; everyone comes up
against it, since it is created by unconscious imitation. It is
nothing but this repeated imitation which gives the illusion of
something concrete: a stumbling-block. One keeps coming back
to it because of the need to assert oneself (the fame of 'Lycidas'),
to be honoured and vindicated. Were it non-existent, one
would create it in order to gain its favour and prestige. Para-
doxically, it is both external and internal, since the obstacle
is the creation of men who precede us, who themselves have
suffered 'that last infirmity of noble mind', and it is internal in
our imitation of the nobility which feeds on fame. We imitate
others so as to seem original in their eyes, and what is imitated
is their desire for recognition.[13] Thus, the obstacle is a repetition
of others, but to repeat others is to displace them, to gain one's
'meed' at their expense, since fame would be meaningless if
all were famous. Opposed to this desire is the equality of
'solemn troops, and sweet Societies / That sing, and singing in

[13] *Cf.* René Girard, *Deceit, Desire, and the Novel: Self and Other in Literary
Structure*, trans. Yvonne Freccero (Baltimore: The Johns Hopkins Press,
1965); and Jacques Lacan, 'The Insistence of the Letter in the Unconscious',
YFS, 36–7 (1966), pp. 137, 143.

their glory move'. The objective in 'Lycidas' is the rejection
of this mechanism of displacement caused by the rivalry for
fame in the acceptance of anonymity in 'sweet Societies' and
the *banality* of the Protestant sermons.[14] Not 'set off to th' world',
but an 'uncouth Swain'.

[14] Don Cameron Allen, *The Harmonious Vision: Studies in Milton's Poetry*
(Baltimore: The Johns Hopkins Press, 1954), pp. 69–70.

4
Advocacy on the 'hill of scandal'

I vehemently inveighed against the egregious ignorance of effrontery of men who professed better things, and from whom better things might have been expected.

Second Defense

> . . . there can be slain
> No sacrifice to god more acceptable
> than an unjust and wicked king. . . .

Seneca, *Hercules Furens*

No society is perfect. Each has within itself, by nature, an impurity, incompatible with the norms to which it lays claim: this impurity finds outlet in elements of injustice, cruelty, and insensitivity.

Lévi-Strauss, *Tristes Tropiques*

Perhaps the most disturbing aspect for Milton in his involvement in the 'grand old cause' was the role of advocate it imposed upon him. As advocate, there evolved the real possibility that Milton would become no better than those he opposed, and that he might become through his words as much a stumbling-block to the faith of others as certain groups, particularly the corrupt clergy, had become for him. For the role of advocate is based on the assumption of the opposition's guilt. Thus it is others, defined as the guilty, who carry the burden and who are sacrificed in order that the righteous can sustain their own beliefs and achieve vindication. *Comus* and 'Lycidas' show, however, that in a situation of violence, there is no way of differentiating good from evil, except through the superimposition of a mythic reading of ambiguous events. Specifically, myths are the creation of the winning side, and their function is to maintain proper distinctions and they do so in such a way as to legitimize the winner and the tactics which led to his victory.

Objectively, in a context of violence, there is no difference between the contending parties: both are contaminated by disputes and equivocations. To maintain a difference is, consequently, to do so from the point of view of either an actual or a desired resolution to the conflict, since the ending is invariably concerned with the defeat and expulsion of the loser. Consequently, while caught up in the debate over the execution of Charles, Milton adopts a role which renders his stance and his cause extremely problematic.

All this is obvious. What is less so is the way in which this role of advocate undercuts Milton's logic. He says, for instance, in *The Tenure of Kings and Magistrates*, that the revolution did not lead to the execution of the king, because a true king 'is a name of dignity and office, not of person'.[1] Rather, Charles is killed for being a counterfeit, since 'the end of a king is for the general good, which he not performing, [he] is but the counterfeit of a king'.[2]

Reason, as the source of Christian liberty, dictates the overthrow of illegitimate rule, and a king's domination is illegitimate if it leads to slavery and the obscuring of reason by empty and idolatrous forms. Milton maintains in *The Tenure* that Charles as king is deposed long before his formal execution; his authority ends at that moment when the Presbyterian leaders began to realize his tyranny and opposed it in both speech and action:

We know that king and subject are relatives, and relatives have no longer being than in relation. The relation between king and subject can be no other than regal authority and subjection. Hence I infer past their defending, that if the subject, who is one relative, take away the relation, of force he takes away also the other relative. But the Presbyterians, who were one relative, that is to say, subjects, have for this seven years taken away the relation, that is to say, the king's authority and their subjection to it. Therefore the Presbyterians for these seven years have removed and extinguished the other relative, that is to say, the king, or, to speak more

[1] Hughes, p. 769.
[2] Hughes, p. 762.

in brief, have deposed him—not only by depriving him the
execution of his authority, but by conferring it upon others.[3]

What Milton expresses here is his understanding of the nature
of covenant.[4] A covenant is a free binding of two parties who
are defined by the roles they assign themselves in the 'relation'. Consequently, the 'relation' is nullified when one of the
parties acts in a way contrary to the role assigned him by the
covenant. We arrive at a picture of Charles as his single worst
enemy, and, in the abstract, of a conviction that Charles, and
no one else, is responsible for the king's execution.

In a similar fashion, that is in keeping to the thesis of 'relation', Milton, in *Eikonoklastes*, was able to discredit the claims
of martyrdom made on the king's behalf:

> In which negative voice to have been cast by the doom of
> war and put to death by those who vanquished him in their
> own defense, he reckons to himself more than a negative
> 'Martyrdom'. But martyrs bear witness to the truth, not to
> themselves: 'If I bear witness of myself,' saith Christ, 'my
> witness is not true.'[5]

In relation to the king, Charles's martyrdom is an attempt at
self-justification, where Christ's death is exemplary of a
universal truth—the justification of others. Moreover, as
Charles's advocates attempt to set the king apart, to justify him
to the world as a martyr to his own cause, Milton finds a
reciprocal instrument of doom and a more encompassing justification in the Old Testament:

> First he pleads that 'no Law of God or man gives to subjects
> any power of judicature without or against him'. Which
> assertion shall be proved in every part to be most untrue.
> The first express law of God given to mankind was that to
> Noah, as a law in general to all the sons of men. And by that
> most ancient and universal law, 'whosoever sheddeth man's
> blood, by man shall his blood be shed,' we find here no
> exception. . . . This in the law of Moses, which came next,
> several times is repeated and in one place remarkably,

[3] Hughes, p. 767.   [4] *Cf*. Hughes, p. 767n.   [5] Hughes, p. 802.

Numbers 35: 'Ye shall take no satisfaction for the life of a
murderer, but he shall surely be put to death: the land cannot be cleansed of the blood that is shed therein,' but by the
blood of him that shed it.[6]

In the uninterrupted conflict of the 1640s, the rhetoric
became perplexing, especially as we find Milton returning to
the mosaic code for justification of acts of retribution and
revenge. Aware of this difficulty, he wrote in *Eikonoklastes*:
'Thus in a graceless age things of highest praise and imitation
under a right name, to make them infamous and hateful to the
people, are miscalled.'[7] This leads to the further recognition
that the disputes 'had almost brought religion to a kind of
trading monopoly'.[8]

Aristotle's *Politics* and the Old Testament could be used to
justify a rebellion, if one wished to be a trader in the currency
of religious symbolism aimed towards the justifications of
political expediency; but the gospels were not as tractable
to the ends of rebellion, with the possible exception of the
eschatological documents. Replying to the charge in *Eikon
Basilike* that the king's judges were also his accusers—that is
to say, the royalist camp seized on the problematic nature of
the role of advocate—Milton's only defence is to envision the
act of judgement as impelled by his involvement in an apocalyptic event:

'It is a sad fate,' saith he, 'to have his enemies both
accusers, parties, and judges.' Sad indeed, but no sufficient
plea to acquit him from being so judged. For what malefactor
might not plead the like? If his own crimes have made all
men his enemies, who else can judge him? They of the powder-
plot against his father might as well have pleaded the same.
Nay at the Resurrection it may as well be pleaded, that the
saints who then shall judge the world, are 'both enemies,
judges, parties, and accusers.[9]

Milton comes close to a defence of the regicide on the grounds
maintained by seventeenth-century zealots and 'enthusiasts',

[6] Hughes, p. 808.   [7] Hughes, p. 787.
[8] Ibid.   [9] Hughes, p. 814.

a group he derides in other circumstances. It is all too easy
to be on the side of the saints, and to perform judgements as
if the apocalypse had arrived.

More convincing and also more in keeping with Milton's
usual method is an argument based on reasonable grounds,
since it was for him the only firm basis of law:

> He himself hath many times acknowledged to have no right
> over us but by law; and by the same law to govern us: but
> law in a free nation hath been ever public reason, the enacted
> reason of a Parliament; which he denying to be our law;
> interposing his own private reason which to us is no law.[10]

Charles is no true king because he places himself above the law.
Therefore, if one shakes off his yoke, it is only in order to substitute the law for his tyranny, a law based on the principle
that 'all men naturally were born free'.[11] Nevertheless, the
drift remains disturbing, as reason becomes in the case of the
regicide but another instrument of revenge.[12]

At base merely another passion, reason seeks its own gratifications in disputations, pamphlets, and in the courts, and it
is this interpretation of reason which allows us to see how
Milton and, more noticeably, his adversaries in the prose
can move from closely reasoned argument to personal invective.
In many of the tracts published during this period, reason is
little more than a mask for accusation, and it is this aspect of
the debates which Milton laments in the *Second Defense*.
Milton's explanation for his participation in the 'drear woods'
of the prose remains interesting:

> This awakened all my attention and my zeal. I saw that a
> way was opening for the establishment of real liberty; that the
> foundation was laying for the deliverance of man from the
> yoke of slavery and superstition; that the principles of
> religion, which were the first objects of our care, would
> exert a salutary influence on the manners and constitution

[10] Hughes, p. 792.
[11] *Tenure*, ed. Hughes, p. 754.
[12] *Cf.* Nietzsche, *Beyond Good and Evil*, Part I, Section 2, in *Basic Writings
of Nietzsche*, ed. and trans. Walter Kaufmann (New York: Modern Library,
1968), pp. 199–201. All further references to Nietzsche are to this edition.

of the republic; and as I had from my youth studied the distinctions between religious and civil rights, I perceived that if I ever wished to be of use, I ought at least not to be wanting to my country, to my church, and to so many of my fellow-Christians, in a crisis of so much danger.[13]

Like the idealism of Elder Brother in *Comus*, Milton's serenity did not last and the debates ultimately led to a transformation of reason into a rhetorical warfare where little remained sacred.

Milton's stance as advocate represents only one side of the prose, and it should be recognized that Milton was aware that even good men can give scandal to others, can sow discord deluded by the strategy of 'an old and perfect enemy'.[14] In general, Milton's intention is conciliatory in the binding of the people together in a free commonwealth. Always ready to stress the 'cheerfulness of the people',[15] their desire for reformation in a 'bond of amity',[16] his objections are against those who would close the way to this new brotherhood. As he writes in *The Tenure*: 'let them not oppose their best friends and associates, who molest them not at all, infringe not the least of their liberties—unless they call it their liberty to bind other men's consciences—but are still seeking to live at peace with them and brotherly accord.'[17] Milton's wrath in *The Tenure* is reserved for the divines who would oppose this ideal: secure in their 'presumptuous Sion', they 'scandalize his (Christ's) church' for the 'filthy love of gain'.[18]

As iconoclast, Milton will tear down the temple of the corrupt clergy by revealing the prelates as 'ravenous wolves'.[19] These are the arts of war and of rebellion as Milton understood them: to fight against external posers whether king, magistrate, or prelate. The fruits of victory, however, bring little satisfaction, if the battle ends with the defeat of these external foes. For once deposed, they are replaced by others no better or worse than they had been. As Milton says in the *Second Defense*: 'they may change their masters, but will never be able to get rid of their servitude'.[20]

Peace can be maintained only with continued effort, as seen

[13] Hughes, p. 830.   [14] Hughes, p. 772.   [15] Hughes, p. 748.
[16] Hughes, p. 761.   [17] Hughes, p. 772.   [18] Hughes, p. 773.
[19] Ibid.   [20] Hughes, p. 837.

in *The Ready and Easy Way* and the exceptional passage from the *Second Defense* where he advises the cultivation of the 'arts of peace':

> If after being released from the toils of war you neglect the arts of peace, if your peace and your liberty be a state of warfare, if war be your only virtue, the summit of your praise, you will, believe me, soon find peace the most adverse to your interests. Your peace will only be a more distressing war, and that which you imagined liberty will prove the worst of slavery. Unless by the means of piety, not frothy and loquacious, but operative, unadulterated, and sincere, you clear the horizon of the mind from those mists of superstition which arise from the ignorance of true religion, you will always have those who will bend your necks to the yoke as if you were brutes, who, notwithstanding all your triumphs, will put you up to the highest bidder as if you were mere booty made in war; and will find an exuberant source of wealth in your ignorance and superstition. Unless you will subjugate the propensity to avarice, to ambition and sensuality, and expel all luxury from yourselves and from your families, you will find that you have cherished a more stubborn and intractable despot at home than you ever encountered in the field; and even your very bowels will be continually teeming with an intolerable progeny of tyrants.[21]

Not rebellion, but revolution; not a deposing of external foes, but a more difficult expelling of 'all luxury from yourselves'. Otherwise, with the war ended, the individual finds himself like Satan at the beginning of *Paradise Lost* or the hero of *Samson Agonistes*, still captive to stronger passions:

> . . . I seek
> This unfrequented place to find some ease;
> Ease to the body some, none to the mind
> From restless thoughts, that like a deadly swarm
> Of Hornets arm'd, no sooner found alone,
> But rush upon me thronging, and present
> Times past, what once I was, and what am now.
>
> (16–22)

[21] Hughes, p. 836.

Samson comes to learn in time that he is his own worst enemy
and transforms himself into an iconoclast in tearing down the
pillars of the temple. This is revolution, an overturning of man's
estate, not through the substitution of other dominations either
external or internal, but by putting an end to the domination
of myths and superstitions enshrined in temples. For Milton,
temples give the appearance of freedom, only, however, that
man may be bound in a greater servitude to a culture which
panders to his passions.

Milton writes at the end of *Areopagitica* that the aim of a
Christian community is to rebuild the temple in the awareness
that the task can never be completed: 'and when every stone is
laid artfully together, it cannot be united into a continuity, it
can but be contiguous in this world; neither can every piece of
the building be of one form; nay rather the perfection consists
in this, that out of many moderate varieties and brotherly
dissimilitudes that are not vastly disproportional, arises the
goodly and graceful symmetry that commends the whole pile
and structure.'[22] Presenting no affront to the eyes of the faithful,
this temple is no living monument to man's pride and luxurious-
ness. On the contrary, it is ever in the making in the Christian
practice and moderation of 'good men'. 'What wants there to
such a towardly and pregnant soul but wise and faithful
labourers to make a knowing people, a nation of prophets, of
sages, and of worthies?'[23] Opposed to the conformity of 'linen
decency',[24] this temple represents a true reformation in a
return to the primitive church:

We read not that Christ ever exercised force but once, and
that was to drive profane ones out of his temple, not to force
them in; and if their being there was an offense, we find by
many other scriptures that their praying there was an
abomination: and yet to the Jewish law, that nation, as a
servant, was obliged; but to the gospel each person is left
voluntary, called only as a son, by the preaching of the word;
not to be driven in by edicts and force of arms. For if by the
apostle (Rom. xii, 1) we are 'beseeched as brethren by the
mercies of God to present' our 'bodies a living sacrifice, holy,
acceptable to God, which is' our 'reasonable service,' or

[22] Hughes, p. 744.   [23] Hughes, p. 743.   [24] Hughes, p. 747.

worship, then is no man to be forced by the compulsive laws
of men to present his body a dead sacrifice, and so under the
gospel most unholy and unacceptable, because it is his
unreasonable service, that is to say, not only unwilling but
unconscionable.[25]

In chasing out the moneylenders, Christ exemplifies the separation of civil and ecclesiastical powers, and any subsequent
joining of the two by those whom Milton calls the 'dancing
divines' represents a transformation of 'the sacred verity of God
to an idol with two faces'.[26]

An even more specific illustration of the scandal and doubleness of an unreformed temple is given in *Means to Remove
Hirelings*: 'and upon her whose only head is in heaven, yea,
upon him who is her only head, sets another in effect, and,
which is most monstrous, a human on a heavenly, a carnal on a
spiritual, a political head on an ecclesiastical; which at length
by such heterogeneal, such incestuous conjunction, transforms
her ofttimes into a beast of many heads and many horns.'[27]
To join church and state is to create the apocalyptic monster of
doubleness which works through deceit and compulsion.

The intermixing of civil with ecclesiastical forms is responsible for the introduction of laws into the domain of religion—
an area which, for Milton, should be without external compulsion. Law, whether religious or civil, signifies compulsion, and,
as Milton says in *Paradise Lost*, law does not erase sin; rather, it
confirms its existence. Compulsion, then, in matters of conscience creates an obstacle to faith: it is the scandal of the false
Sion. Further, Milton writes, ' "That which justifies not in the
gospel, condemns," or, in other words (Rom. xiv, 23), "Whatso-
ever is not of faith, is sin." '[28] Any other method than that of
faith, for Milton, stands for closure and mystification in the
idol-worship of the double. Thus, as iconoclast, his function is
to reveal the monstrosity, that is to say, the doubleness, created
by the law as a product of 'incestuous conjunction'.

Milton, in his prose defences of the commonwealth, can be
judged by his own best principles, and, following this course, he
might be found contradictory and responsive to the compulsion

---

[25] Hughes, p. 853.   [26] Hughes, p. 753.
[27] Hughes, pp. 872–3.   [28] Hughes, p. 852.

of his own double standard. For Milton, justice, insofar as justice is reason, depends on *discerning* the correspondence of Charles's fate to what had been prophesied in the Bible as the consequence of a tyranny which fed on innocent blood. Such is the intent of the epigram which introduces *Eikonoclastes*: 'A man that doth violence to the blood of any person, shall fly to the pit, let no man stay him,' (Prov. xxviii, 17).[29] The Bible attests to the circularity of human endeavour: judgement taken will rebound on the accuser, blood spilt will be repaid. Thus, the law ultimately imprisons the law-giver if he follows his own inclination and passion.

The redundancy of the positive law is countered by the spontaneity of 'natural law' which is based on reason.[30] Interestingly, it is the mixture of the two in 'incestuous conjoining' (of freedom and compulsion) which creates scandal and is exactly the obstacle to worship and community which Milton emphasized throughout his prose and which he characterized as 'Babel' religion where words become 'cyphers' to be interchanged in the market-place of public opinion. Conformity simply serves to hide a variety of unconforming sins, since 'truth and understanding are not such wares as to be monopolized and traded in by tickets and statutes and standards. We must not think to make a staple commodity of all the knowledge in the land, to mark and license it like our broadcloth and our wool packs.'[31] And, in another example taken from *Areopagitica* where Milton shows the 'publican' as blind to the nature of Christian truth as a 'streaming fountain':

A wealthy man addicted to his pleasure and to his profits, finds religion to be a traffic so entangled, and of so many piddling accounts, that of all mysteries he cannot skill to keep a stock going upon that trade. What should he do? Fain he would have the name to be religious, fain he would bear up with his neighbours in that. What does he, therefore, but resolves to give over toiling and to find himself out some

29 Hughes, p. 781.
30 Milton's conception of positive versus natural law is similar to Lévi-Strauss's emphasis of the nature / culture opposition in *The Elementary Structures of Kinship* (Paris: Presses Universitaire de France, 1949). *Cf.* Jacques Derrida, 'Structure, Sign, and Play', in *The Languages of Criticism*, p. 253.   31 Hughes, pp. 736–7.

factor to whose care and credit he may commit the whole managing of his religious affairs; some Divine of note and estimation that must be. To him he adheres, resigns the whole warehouse of his religion with all the locks and keys into his custody; and indeed makes the very person of that man his religion; esteems his associating with him a sufficient evidence and commendatory of his own piety. So that a man may say his religion is now no more within himself, but is become a dividual movable, and goes and comes near him, according as that good man frequents the house. He entertains him, gives him gifts, feasts him, lodges him. His religion comes home at night, prays, is liberally supped, and sumptuously laid to sleep, rises, is saluted, and after the malmsey, or some well spiced brewage, and better breakfasted than he whose morning appetite would have gladly fed on green figs between Bethany and Jerusalem, his religion walks abroad at eight, and leaves his kind entertainer in the shop trading all day without his religion.[32]

In passages like this, we discover ('laughter also is reason') the nature of those stones which will make up the building of the temple, 'not continuous, but contiguous in this world', and the domestic source of superstition and tyranny. We also learn in this passage that culture (different from the culture expounded in Of Education) is the proliferation of scandal in the habits of self-indulgence.

A culturally acceptable religion is no true religion for Milton, but despotism which functions through the use of a rudimentary technology in transforming the spiritual individuality of the sacramental wine into the Bacchic degeneracy of wholesale religion. The Word, no longer a call to community ('By love serve one another' (Gal. v, 13)), enters the province of public relations, and, in the end, serves to accelerate competition and discord: no longer the sense of language as a source of debate and reformation, but the secret oppression of the secularized word.[33] Milton's task, consequently, was to destroy

[32] Hughes, pp. 739–40.
[33] When T. S. Eliot referred to Milton's unfortunate influence on the language of the seventeenth century, he failed to realize that Milton was fully conscious of possessing an instrument which had been previously

the idols of the market place in showing that the double standard, as with all doubles, is the product of a subjective desire for
domination in the proliferation of rivalries whether domestic or
foreign.

Out of idol worshipping comes the cult of the hero (in a
Greek context, the cult of the hero is the creation of a city
society)[34] and an attendant increase in discord and warfare.
This mechanism, however, goes against the best interests of the
state, since as Jean-Pierre Vernant said: 'The ideal of the City is
for citizens to be equal, whereas the heroic ideal is to be always
first.'[35] It is this difference and the desire promulgating the
'heroic ideal' which must be expelled from the city, and it is to
this end that Milton's prose writing is directed. In the words
of the *Second Defense*:

> When the bishops could no longer resist the multitude of
> their assailants, I had leisure to turn my thoughts to other
> subjects, to the promotion of real and substantial liberty,
> which is rather to be sought from within than from without,
> and whose existence depends not so much on the terror of the
> sword as on sobriety of conduct and integrity of life.[36]

The concept of community as a rational assembly of individuals
exceptional in their attempt to forge a life based on 'sobriety
of conduct and integrity' is at the centre of all that Milton did.

In this respect, *Paradise Lost* can be seen as an anatomy and
celebration of community, a celebration, that is, as long as the
community remains free of the effects of idolatry. The Satanic
fall is related to the rejection of a new community offered to the
angels in heaven, described by Abdiel as intended 'to exalt /
Our happy state under one Head more near / United' (V,
830–31). In opposition to this community, Satan sets up his
own kingdom in hell, which he believes is more equitable than
that of heaven. Neither community, however, is intended as a
human model, since both are the product of inhuman laws in
the precise sense that they are not of this world, and that

---

contaminated and that his method was reflective in the double sense of
mirroring and elucidation.

[34] Jean-Pierre Vernant, 'Greek Tragedy: Problems of Interpretation', in
The Languages of Criticism, p. 283.

[35] Vernant, 'Greek Tragedy', p. 283.   [36] Hughes, p. 830.

both (not only hell) are constructed according to a system of idolatry.

At the centre of *Paradise Lost*, the Garden represents a new model of community which is broken prior to the fall when Eve separates from Adam in order that they may improve their cultivation. As a result, Adam and Eve, like Satan, become for a time 'alienate from God' (V, 877) in their exclusion from community. But even the Garden as image of community is suspect, because it stands for an ambiguous condition: good, insofar as it calls for union and harmony, and evil, to the extent that harmony is achieved by idolatry, the particular idolatry inherent in Adam's desire to play God with his mate. Eve's separation from Adam follows from her wish to be equal with Adam and to escape his tyranny, and, in this sense, it exemplifies her defiance of hierarchical order. If the poem is successful, it will require the resolution of this conflict, so that Adam and Eve can truly be said to be 'homeward returning' (XII, 632) at the end of the poem—returning, that is, to a home free from tyranny and superstition.

There is another dimension to the epic which relates to this analysis of the prose and this concerns the staging of the role of advocate in the character of Satan and, in a more indirect fashion, as an aspect of the stance of the narrator. The advocate, we learn in *Paradise Lost*, stands against the judges, as Satan stands against the Father's justice, but the immediate result of his taking this stand is to render his enterprise contradictory. This is best shown in Satan's soliloquies, in the obstacles he encounters in his journey to the earth, and his subsequent temptations of Eve. Satan seeks vindication and achieves his purpose by transforming Adam and Eve into victims. This would appear to be his final justification. yet, its final effect is to confirm the inclusiveness of God's Word and justice, a providence which extends beyond Satan's subjective aspirations. Thus the Satanic experience reflects on Milton's activity in the prose, but as Satan is merely an aspect of the larger intentions of the epic, *Paradise Lost* represents a step beyond and outside the contagion of prose warfare.

Paradise Lost is a meta-text of pamphlets like *Eikonoklastes* and *The Ready and Easy Way*; in terms of Milton's own experience, *Paradise Lost* is words about words and an intermixing of his early thoughts and hopes and their later disconfirmations. How do we situate ourselves in a meta-text and what do we know in a context without beginnings and endings? At first sight, what we find is that the labyrinth of the meta-text is antidote to the advocacy of the prose in the sense that the prose experience is understood as both a loss and, more importantly, as a situation of being lost in the mazy labyrinth of doubling words. At what point was one outside the labyrinth and what certainty can one find when convinced that even though there may have been a point of entry, it is in the past and that, for now, all one can do is deal with the origin from the confusion of the labyrinth? It is not, then, a question of escaping the labyrinth—even this pos- sibility is included in the constitution of the labyrinth—but of realizing that the meta-text only records repetitions. As in Milton's prose, we discover while lost in the labyrinth that we often return to the same junctures and these repetitions allow us to discover the pattern of the labyrinth. Thus, *Paradise Lost*, as a commentary on the prose and as its own proper confusion 'in wandering mazes lost', must be seen in terms of repetitions. The existing pattern is always experienced too late, but, given this, it is, nevertheless, experienced. In a way, *Paradise Lost*, as opposed to Milton's pamphlets with their certainty both of reason and mission, is an act of deferred meaning: it is an action which follows the perilous trace of the word or, in the context of Book XII, it is an act 'informing them by types / And shadows' (232–3). It is a message which must be lived through if it is to have any meaning. It is typology, but it is also the particular typology of the seventeenth century—typo- logy set to type. In any event, it is given to us to understand, while reading *Paradise Lost*, what Borges meant when he wrote: 'Tlon is surely a labyrinth, but it is a labyrinth devised by men, destined to be deciphered by men.'

PART II
The human epic

5
The maze of interpretation

> It is true that the most ancient men, the first librarians, used a language quite different from the one we now speak; it is true that a few miles to the right the tongue is dialectical and that ninety floors farther up, it is incomprehensible.
>
> Borges, 'The Library of Babel'

(i) Imitation

Many of the issues raised in the preceding pages are re-examined in *Paradise Lost*; yet Milton's epic need not be seen as an overt attempt at justification, whatever the cause, or as a didactic instrument, not that a message cannot be extracted from the poem, as Raphael and Michael—along with an assorted crew of 'angelic' critics—teach us in their narratives. It is much too easy, even though the truth is ever 'plain and perspicacious'.[1] Rather, the most easily grasped 'truth' of *Paradise Lost* is a misdirection insofar as it is little more than the validation of the law, a law which was seen as responsible for the proliferation of 'doubleness' in the prose. Moreover, in the words of *Areopagitica*, 'if it come to prohibiting, there is not aught more likely to be prohibited than truth itself; whose first appearance to our eyes bleared and dimmed with prejudice and custom, is more unsightly and unplausible than many errors, even as the person is of many a great man slight and contemptible to see to'.[2]

Oversensitive to the idolatrous nature of the Satanic way, it is also easy to ignore the fact that God can also become an idol, when he is employed to create division and discord. Ever an iconoclast in the most radical sense of the word, Milton,

[1] *Cf.* Milton's statement on truth as teaching in *Eikonoklastes*, Hughes, p. 807.
[2] Hughes, p. 748.

in *Paradise Lost*, sets out to demonstrate that God's purpose (God, in this sense, is the first iconoclast) is his own eradication before man's freedom. Adam and Eve, in short, must awaken from God's dream before they can become free and human, since for Milton, it is freedom which defines the human. For, God's ways are unnatural, or, more precisely, his ways, according to Borges, are 'inhuman'. To imitate God is to become inhuman, a monster among men. Adam, imitating his interview with God in Book VIII, learns this when he attempts to play God with Eve: he is transformed into a monster. To be saved, he must, by contrast, come to respect Eve's independence, her singularity, and only after his transformation can they unite again 'hand in hand', not 'continuous, but contiguous'.

If we are to understand *Paradise Lost*, we must begin with its ending and give full emphasis to its last words: 'thir solitary way'. Adam and Eve must fashion their new life without divine intercession, since God's gift to man was his own willing sacrifice, a sacrifice which is in exact terms the killing of his image in Christ and, consequently, of the force of any idols (again, there is no distinction between divine and the Satanic idols) over the behaviour of men. In this way, Adam and Eve are free to act in a human community of 'single, just men'. One is almost tempted to say, in contradiction to C. S. Lewis, who categorically states that *Paradise Lost* can only be understood by a good Christian, that only through a radical Christian position verging on heresy, if not atheism, can one begin to value the real import of the epic: God is dead that man may live.[3]

In the *Aeneid*, to take an example which undoubtedly had a substantial impact on Milton's achievement, we find a similar rejection of the gods, particularly as portrayed in the tragic fate of the Homeric Turnus. Yet, the place of the gods, as Brooks Otis argues, is taken by Aeneas, 'in effect, an Augustan type—a *divine man*, not necessarily copied after the Emperor himself but embodying the Augustan ruler-ideal—who emerges out of Homeric society and, in virtue of his emergence, imposes upon a more primitive but still quasi-Homeric society a defeat that is the means to unity, peace and civilization on the

---

[3] C. S. Lewis, *A Preface to Paradise Lost* (London: Oxford University Press, 1942), p. 136.

Augustan plan'.[4] One is unlikely, however, to mistake Adam for Aeneas, not that he does not learn to subordinate his *furor* and *impietas* to an ideal of community, but rather because in Adam's world fate no longer functions to guarantee the ascendency of the righteous. On the contrary, Virgil's 'ruler-ideal' is subverted by Milton as the stereotype of the ruler becomes Nimrod at the beginning of Book XII. Described by Otis as 'in a word . . . a civilized poet',[5] Virgil celebrates the prospect of a unified and peaceful world under the benevolent rule of Rome, where Milton renders the hypostasis of empire building in the image of Babel: 'thus was the building left / Ridiculous, and the work Confusion nam'd' (XII, 61–2). If Virgil is civilized, what then is Milton? Are we to find a model in his Adam? Assuredly, in Adam we find a general model of fall, repentance, regeneration, and hope. What does this mean, however, in terms of his practical behaviour?

Adam is a singularly unsatisfying 'character'. This, perhaps, explains why so many critics are drawn to Satan. Extrapolating from the text, our overall impression of Adam concerns his inadequacy in the Garden. For one thing, he is never allowed to act in the Garden; when he does, it is a crucial blunder. Rather, he talks and postures (especially with Eve). When not talking to Eve, he appears to lack awareness of his purpose in the Garden; the word 'wandering', often employed to describe Satanic activity, seems particularly apt in describing Adam. Alone in the Garden, he is dissatisfied, and it is this feeling which prompts his request for Eve. Pleased with his new possession, he is counselled by Raphael to undervalue this gift.

With respect to Raphael's narrative of the 'War in Heaven', he is dumbfounded and obviously learns little from it, since shortly he will fall to his own idol-worship in following Eve's example. After the fall, and, importantly, after having made up with Eve, he again is taken by the hand and given a fairly detailed instruction concerning his future and the sort of behaviour expected from him. But to what purpose, since his

---

[4] *Virgil: A Study in Civilized Poetry* (Oxford: Clarendon Press, 1964), p. 384. Professor Michael Bristol supplied this reference and was extremely helpful when I began this chapter.

[5] Otis, p. 393.

individual reformation will seemingly have no application to this world, but to that which follows the Second Coming? We begin to see the point of 'thir solitary way'. There may be a pattern somewhere 'out there'; for now, however, what characterizes the individual quest in day to day terms is its idiosyncratic nature. Adam is no hero; on the contrary, he is all too familiar, a bungler like ourselves. Obviously, little satisfaction is meant to be taken in this portrayal.

Indeed, the weak will subvert the strong; not weakness, however, as a mystified version of the apocalyptic victory of the 'saints', but weakness as understood in terms of everyday failings, the imperfections which belong to both master and slave. What will overthrow the hero is his own weakness, his vanity and self-love, as Milton emphasizes in the prose where he suggests that true mastery is from within, as it is from within that one achieves integrity and strength. Adam is no model, then, as every reader must go his solitary way after the book closes.[6]

Exception must be taken with Dr Johnson's belief that the 'plan of *Paradise Lost* . . . comprises neither human actions nor human manners. The man and woman who act and suffer, are in a state which no other man or woman can ever know. The reader finds no transaction in which he can be engaged; beholds no condition in which he can by any effort of imagination place himself; he has, therefore, little natural curiosity or sympathy.'[7] It is difficult to know exactly what Dr Johnson intends by this statement, how he reached this conclusion, and, moreover, how he could have failed to notice that Adam and Eve are a true reflection of the reader. As mirror images of the reader, they do no doubt present problems, especially if a reader insists on a flattering reflection. As to the additional charge that the reader of *Paradise Lost* 'finds no transaction in which he can be engaged', it seems that this charge can be directed against any art which is not plainly mimetic.[8] To do

[6] See Stanley Fish, *Surprised by Sin* (London: Macmillan, 1967); and particularly, his discussion of the 'guilty reader' and the critical consensus on this theme, p. 2.

[7] 'The Lives of the English Poets' in *Milton Criticism: Selections from Four Centuries*, ed. James Thorpe (New York: Collier, 1950), p. 80.

[8] It could be argued that Blake's admiration for Milton was based on his recognition of the visionary quality of *Paradise Lost* and the manner in which

so, however, is to ignore the specific issues raised by this technique. Nevertheless, Dr Johnson's observations remain useful, if only to point to the particular problems raised by *Paradise Lost*. He continues:

> Another inconvenience of Milton's design is that it requires the description of what cannot be described, the agency of spirits. He saw that immateriality supplied no images, and that he could not show angels acting but by instruments of action; he therefore invested them with form and matter. This, being necessary, was therefore defensible; and he should have secured the consistency of his system, by keeping immateriality out of sight, and enticing his reader to drop it from his thoughts.[9]

The observation is justified, the conclusion less so. It could as easily be argued that, the classical rules aside, the only way Milton could achieve his purpose was through highlighting the inconsistency of spirit and matter. Dr Johnson is demanding that Milton reproduce the *Aeneid*, and, consequently, he misses the originality of Milton's poem, much as the early imitators of Homer failed to write credible epics in their slavish copying of the original. Virgil's originality lay not in imitation, but in exploitation. Understanding the epic form better than his predecessors, Virgil was able to incorporate the epic material of Homer to his own ends.[10] It is our contention that such was Milton's objective: 'to soar / Above the *Aonian* Mount.'

Returning to Dr Johnson's observations, the point that Milton is representing characters who never existed, or that certain characters 'require the description of what cannot be described', it can be argued that they support the claim that *Paradise Lost* represents a radical rejection of the theory of imitation, and, to the extent that this is so, it, in turn, undermines the possibility of the text as didactic instrument. An encyclopedic undertaking, the function of Milton's poem is paradoxical: the aim of including exhaustive information on

---

it subverted the mimetic requirements of eighteenth-century art. I differ, however, from Blake's judgement in *Milton* that the vision was an unconscious production and that Milton was unaware of its meaning.

[9] *The Lives of the English Poets*, ed. Thorpe, pp. 81–2.
[10] See Otis, 'The Obsolescence of Epic', pp. 5–40.

any given topic seems, finally, to prove that knowledge is useless, especially as this knowledge pertains to externals.[11]

The treatment of the 'outward' paradise in Eden is lengthy, amplified with numerous 'artificial' devices, while the 'Paradise within' is given scant attention. The artificial and outward Paradise is lost, and we are intended to know, as a result of its extended description, exactly what it is we lose; what we gain is less easy to know, except in the negative sense in which it is something other than the Garden of Eden, transformed as it is into an 'Island salt and bare' (XI, 834), after the flood.

The images are destroyed at the end of *Paradise Lost*. but, then, they had never been particularly secure, because the narrator is living after the fact and merely records as scribe inspired by his muse, the dismembered body of the fallen word.[12] Thus, it becomes part of the Satanic method to foster belief in the image and its capability to persuade for the sake of reformation; Satan is didactic and will exhort his defeated and reluctant legions with the image as prod.[13] Milton, on the other hand, will imitate 'the careful search that Isis made for the mangled body of Osiris',[14] but one should remember that, in this life, at least, the search ends in failure as those images left standing are there to commemorate human defeat and subjugation.

It is interesting that those critics (Waldock comes to mind) who appreciate Satan are also those who seek in *Paradise Lost* a 'well told story', with a straight plot development and fully realized characters. Milton, on the contrary, takes great pains to break the narrative, to create enigmatic fragments, and to destroy the possibility of extended identifications, a technique which is again directed to the abolishing of the kind of imitation which ultimately is seen as subjection. Satan exemplifies this alternative extremely well in his doomed imitation of God, since it is one which simply serves to increase his anguish and to secure his bondage. We will have the opportunity, later in this study, to examine the one story in the epic which is

---

[11] Northrop Frye, *The Return of Eden* (Toronto: University of Toronto Press, 1965), p. 109.

[12] *Areopagitica*, ed. Hughes, pp. 741–2.

[13] *Cf.* John Steadman, 'Milton's Rhetoric: Satan and the "Unjust Discourse"', *MS*, I (1969), pp. 67–92.

[14] *Areopagitica*, ed. Hughes, p. 742.

recounted in a straightforward manner (even here, however, a critic given over to realism and 'consistency' can find grounds for faulting the development insofar as the passage intermingles 'spirit' and 'matter'), a story which is prefaced by Raphael's well-known Platonic instruction concerning the problems implicit in the conception of art as imitation. For the time being, however, we can say that in the 'War in Heaven', the Platonic directive is intended: (1) to delimit the force of the presentation; and, (2) to suggest the possibility that the source of inspiration in this passage is not an atemporal world of forms but this world of contention and partisanship: 'though what if Earth / Be but the shadow of Heav'n, and things therein / Each to other like, more than on Earth is thought?' (V, 574-6). In speaking of the gods, in portraying them in 'corporeal form', they appear as little better than men. Because of this, the imitation makes us suspect that the gods are unattractive as a result of having been created by men to represent human discord and violence.

Yet, more disturbing about the 'War in Heaven' is its mythic and self-validating form: the fact that it concludes with the apparition of the Son as the avenging spirit of the Father. But, as the interchanges between the Father and the Son attest, this device was never meant to be taken seriously. It is all a game, or, more to the point, it is a ritual where the outcome is known beforehand—no real game where victory remains in doubt to the end.[15] The 'War in Heaven' introduces Satan, a known quantity, so that he can be expelled at the end, thus justifying by a sleight of hand, the reigning ideology. Involved in the war, Abdiel, naturally, is unaware of this and sees the combat as 'deadly' serious, but the Father and Son, through their lack of 'decorum', signal to us that the ritual is played out, that, indeed, it has become melodrama. The Son, as image, the 'resplendant mirror of the Father', puts an end to the Homeric play acting. It is fitting that what undermines imitation is the specific product of imitation, the image itself.

Christ, as image, undermines his own 'individuality' (the

[15] For a discussion of the interrelationship of rituals and games, see Claude Lévi-Strauss, *The Savage Mind* (Chicago: University of Chicago Press, 1969), pp. 30-33.

term, individuality, is itself questionable, as Milton's version
of the trinity depicts the Son as a form of emanation; in any
case, he is hardly an independent agent of the divine purpose)
by fulfilling his Father's desire. Beyond this, however, insofar
as the Son is the 'true image' of the Father, he exemplifies that
the image is grounded on a faithful imitation, that is to say,
that as image, the Son is thoroughly determined by a prior
imitation. This is his 'dependency', as it had been that of the
angels before him. Thus, as the Son is meant to illustrate the
nature of the relationships in Heaven as grounded in imitation
and 'dependency', it is also possible to interpret him, as Satan
does, as an obstacle to a worship which is thought to be
grounded in the freedom of love: Satan 'could not bear /
Through pride that sight, and thought himself impaired' (V,
664–5). What Satan refuses to recognize is that worship and
love are, at base, imitation and dependency. Once aware of
this, he 'thought himself impaired' and transforms the recuperative agency of love into a debilitating rivalry, 'yet
fraught / With envy against the Son of God' (V, 661–2).

Christ's sacrifice, on the other hand, reveals that true liberty
follows from the recognition that the only liberty possible is to
accomplish the Father's will. Any other way is to be reduced to
Satan's contradictions, 'all Good to me is lost; / Evil be thou
my Good' (IV, 109–10), and to a transformation, equally self-
defeating, of love into envy and of imitation into rivalry. For,
as René Girard has shown in his analysis of *Oedipus Rex*, at the
root of imitation is the potential for rivalry, since in imitating
another, one imitates his desire, a desire which is directed to a
particular object.[16] This double desire for the same object
gives birth to rivalry, and rivalry, in turn, has the effect of
transforming what would otherwise be but another mundane
object into an image of surpassing worth: the prerogatives of
kingship, the sacramental throne, and the magical power
secretly locked in the king's sceptre. This interpretation allows
us to see that it is Satan, through his perverted desire, who
transforms God into a tyrannical king in his mystification and
transformation of God's supremacy into the icons of power.
Not surprisingly, these icons which clothe Christ on the last

[16] 'Symétrie et Dissymétrie dans le Mythe d'Oedipe', p. 127.

day of battle in the 'War of Heaven' defeat Satan and his crew:

> Full soon
> Among them he arriv'd; in his right hand
> Grasping ten thousand Thunders, which he sent
> Before him, such as thir Soul's infix'd
> Plagues; they astonisht all resistance lost,
> All courage; down thir idle weapons dropp'd;
> O'er Shields and Helms, and helmed heads he rode
> Of Thrones and mighty Seraphim prostrate,
> That wish't the Mountains now might be again
> Thrown on them as a shelter from his ire.
>
> (VI, 834–44)

Christ's power is as much the creation of the rebellious angels— they have transformed him into an image of wrath through their envy—as it is the delegated strength of the Father. 'Ten thousand Thunders' is a natural metaphor for the Son's power, but also it represents the violence of the angels, locked in deadly combat, a violence which will guarantee their defeat as surely as the impious rulers of Egypt, in *Exodus*, called down divine wrath through the violence which they did to God's 'chosen people'.[17] It is not the Son who 'infix'd / Plagues' so much as the rebel angels, who, having set out to 'contaminate' (with discord) the holy harmony of Heaven, discover that the contagion which they set loose has rebounded on themselves as its authors. The Son simply serves to reveal this reciprocity, and in the 'revelation' is their doom.

(ii) So many words

The circularity and reciprocity of violence stems from the Satanic interpretation of the Word: the attempt to defeat the Word with other words, and, to undercut the Word through action. Action in the 'War in Heaven', however, is little more than words, exemplified by the traditional fliting of Homeric

---

[17] *Cf.* René Girard, 'Dionysos et la Genèse Violente du Sacré', *Poétique*, III (1970), pp. 348–64.

battle. Everything in *Paradise Lost* is anchored in words. Our
initial impression of particular events in the poem may give the
sense of their being a response to earlier events, and this may
create the impression that these actions can be traced back to an
originating event at the root of language, but, in this impression, we are partly mistaken. What is given, rather, is a recounting of incidents through language; nothing is seen at first-hand.
The original action, for that matter, is largely a literary event
in the creation of an image, the specific symbolic function of the
Son. Involved in this linguistic context, Satan wishes to strip
away the corrupting gloss of language and to reduce words to
their grounding in things. His activity, in this respect, is that of a
literary critic, and his aim is both to understand and, finally,
to destroy the 'Word made flesh'. Equally, Satan functions as a
poet who would transform an earlier and more 'primitive'
literature which he conceives of as the didactic instrument of a
tyrant into a visionary vehicle which will express his consciousness of things. The aims of both criticism and literature,
however, can be recognized as similar, in that they are directed
to the destruction and condemnation of the Father's value
system. In any case, whether Satan's discourse is literature or
criticism,[18] it all comes down to the same thing: 'language and
the single problematic it imposes, namely, that of interpretation'.[19]

Expanding our discussion of the linguistic nature of the
Satanic predicament, it can be seen that Dr Johnson touched on
the difficulty of *Paradise Lost* when he concentrated his critique
on the nature of the sign in Milton's text, the fact that signs
have no apparent reference to things. In *Paradise Lost*, according
to Dr Johnson, Milton 'saw Nature, as Dryden expresses it,
through the spectacle of books'.[20] The relevance of this observation
goes beyond the purely extrinsic considerations of Milton's
sources, for it underlines the internal problems which face
many of the characters. Examine, for instance, the debate
between Satan and Abdiel, prior to the 'War in Heaven':
Abdiel accepts as true the account of the Son's original creation.

[18] See Eugenio Donato, 'The Two Languages of Criticism', in *The
Languages of Criticism*, pp. 95–6; and '*Tristes Tropiques*: The Endless Journey',
MLN, 81 (1966), pp. 282–5.
[19] Donato, 'The Two Languages of Criticism', p. 96.
[20] *The Lives of the English Poets*, ed. Thorpe, p. 77.

Satan's rebuttal is well known:

> who saw
> When this creation was? remembers't thou
> Thy making, while the Maker gave thee being?
> We know no time when we were not as now;
>
> (V, 856–9)

All that Satan has to go on in this case is faith, and faith means
taking someone's *word*. Edward Said writes, concerning another
example, Raphael's justification of his narrative:

> We may take comfort in Raphael's assertion that there had
> been a *Word*, a primal unity of truth, to which such puzzles
> as 'meaning' and 'reference' are impertinent. Yet, on the
> other hand, we have only his *word* for it; not a thing cer-
> tainly, and not more than an assertion that depends on
> other words and an accepted sense-giving code for
> support.[21]

We can begin to appreciate Satan's literary project of fitting
facts to theory, word to thing.[22] His journey to the earth is, in
addition, but an attempt at verifying God's pronouncements
referred to as the *rumour* of heaven. Finding confirmation of the
rumour, 'here *matter* new to gaze the Devil met' (III, 614,
my emphasis), 'like a devilish Engine back recoils / Upon
himself; horror and doubt distract / His troubled thoughts . . .'
(IV, 17–19). He finds his answer, concludes his interpretation,
only to uncover his own damnation. That is to say that what
lies behind interpretation is nothing more or less than the
interpreter. Interpretation is not an objective search for
confirmation of words by facts, but it is, more nearly, an
expression of the desire to dominate a controversy, of having
one's own word taken over another's.

It is this aspect of interpretation that was referred to in the
discussion of the ambiguity of Milton's prose insofar as Milton

---

[21] 'Abecedarium Culturae: Structuralism, Absence, Writing', *Tri-
Quarterly*, 20 (1971), p. 34.

[22] Armand Himy, 'Milton et la Sortie de la caverne', *Critique*, August
1970, p. 721. He describes Satan's objective as the obverse of Don Quixote
in his quest for similarity.

defended a particular form of domination against another in terms of an a priori truth. Satan, finding that the earth substantiates the *Word*, realizes that his rebellion is not directed to establishing a new freedom, that it is merely a guise for his desire to dominate in Heaven. Setting out to prove God in the wrong, he discovers himself as the guilty one in his soliloquy at the beginning of Book IV. He rationalizes, after this confirmation, that he had had no choice, that if he had been an inferior angel, another, above him 'would have aspir'd, and me though mean / Drawn to his part' (IV, 62–3). While acting in the belief that his only desire is to achieve freedom for himself and his followers, his behaviour has a certain heroic cast (it can be maintained that until Book IV Satan is not aware of his contradictory stance, neither is he aware of the 'real' power of the Father and the Son—he interprets the Son's power in the 'War in Heaven' as a clever strategem, like his creation of artillery—since, when God's power is shown, it dazzles and blinds all who behold), but after the soliloquy on Mount Niphates, his situation is drastically altered as he continues to act as if he were free. At this point, his actions begin to betray him as he enacts in a material setting his own peculiar bondage. Once pure spirit, he is transformed into procreant matter as he becomes a place ('Myself am Hell'), a thing, assorted animals, and, finally, a serpent, the animal who travels on the ground, full prone. For Milton, no doubt, this sequence of transformations is intended to illustrate the source of the various pagan associations with the earth in vegetation rites and natural religion.

The world is Satan's kingdom, because he is all earth, and this is the sign of his fate as it is the grounding from which 'fate' arises. Like the natural cycle, Satan is fated to endless and meaningless repetition, the prototype and source of the Christian understanding of original sin. Thus, original sin is a metaphor for human destiny conceived as compulsive repetition, and, moreover, of a repetition drawn to the flesh which is formed out of earth. As Adam says as he considers his own original sin:

> if Death
> Consort with thee, Death is to me as Life;

> So forcibly within my heart I feel
> The Bond of Nature draw me to my own, . . .
>
> (IX, 953–6)

These sentiments, however fine, will also be subverted as he discovers his 'sentence' and is returned to the dust from which he arose.

Nevertheless, in the pre-fallen state, word and thing are consonant, as illustrated by the 'Morning Prayer' of Book V, where worship resounds the creation, where voice is echoed in things, and in the innate ability of Adam to name the animals. What underlies Adam's innocence is exactly this adequacy of words to things. This state of affairs will continue as long as Adam and Eve remain faithful to the single interdiction of the Garden; their obedience, founded on trust, guarantees that their words will ring true.

This perfect coincidence of words and things, what Said refers to as 'the primal unity of truth', is not without complication even in the Garden, since, as many readers of *Paradise Lost* have noticed, the experience of the Garden is mediated for the reader; mediated, that is, by the Satanic vision which we are made to share. For we descend Mount Nephates with Satan and see Adam and Eve for the first time through his eyes (the narrator's description of Eden, in this respect, seems to be but an extension of the Satanic point of view).[23]

Satan's first action is perfectly consistent with the plan we have thus far outlined; overhearing Adam and Eve discussing their status in the Garden, he devises his first temptation in terms of another testing of the *logos* through the inspiration of Eve's dream:

> him there they found
> Squat like a Toad, close at the ear of *Eve*;
> Assaying by his Develish art to reach
> The Organs of her Fancy, and with them forge
> Illusions as he list, Phantasms and Dreams,

[23] *Cf.* William G. Riggs, 'The Poet and Satan in *Paradise Lost*', *MS*, II (1970), pp. 59–82; and Harry Berger, '*Paradise Lost* Evolving: Books I–VI', *CR*, XI (1967), pp. 483–531.

> Or if, inspiring venom, he might taint
> Th' animal spirits that from pure blood arise
> Like gentle breaths from Rivers pure, thence raise
> At least distemper'd, discontented thoughts,
> Vain hopes, vain aims, inordinate desires
> Blown up with high conceits ingend'ring pride.
>
> (IV, 799-809)

The force of the temptation is to transform Eve into a Petrarchan mistress,[24] 'blown up with high conceits', or, as Eve un-
derstands it from her dream: 'be henceforth among the
Gods / Thyself a Goddess' (V, 77-8). This is interesting in
terms of the description of the first couple just prior to the
temptation as 'these two / Imparadis't in one another's arms'
(IV, 505-6), where there is no need 'the putting off / These
troublesome disguises which we wear' (IV, 739-40), and the
situation which holds shortly after the dream when Raphael
descends to the Garden:

> O innocence
> Deserving Paradise! if ever, then,
> Then had the Sons of God excuse to have been
> Enamourr'd at that sight; but in those hearts
> Love unlibidinous reign'd, nor jealousy
> Was understood, the injur'd Lover's Hell.
>
> (V, 445-50)

In this context, it becomes clear that Satan's temptation is, in
fact, a courtly seduction once he views Eve and falls in love
with her, setting the pattern for the story in Genesis VI, 2-4,
of the sons of Seth who came to be known as the 'sons of God',
a story supported by the interpretation of Augustine and
Aquinas that the lovers of Cain's daughters were fallen angels.[25]
In this sense, Milton integrates the Petrarchan conceits into
his Biblical narrative.

Beyond this, however, is the fact that the love lyrics of the

---

[24] Jackson Cope, *The Metaphoric Structure of Paradise Lost* (Baltimore: The
Johns Hopkins Press, 1962), p. 137.
[25] *Cf.* XI, 573-627; and Hughes's commentary on the passage, p. 446n.

Renaissance and the temptations of Satan have in common
their perversion of language through the satisfaction of
'libidinous' passions. Consequently, their products are similar;
the creation of 'Fancy'. Adam's difficulty in responding to Eve's
dream stems from the fact that Eve's words have no apparent
grounding in things:

> But know that in the Soul
> Are many lesser Faculties that serve
> Reason as chief; among these Fancy next
> Her office holds; of all external things,
> Which the five watchful Senses represent,
> She forms Imaginations, Aery shapes,
> Which Reason joining or disjoining, frames
> All that we affirm or what deny, and call
> Our knowledge or opinion; then retires
> Into her private Cell when Nature rests,
> Oft in her absence mimic Fancy wakes
> To imitate her; but misjoining shapes,
> Wild work produces oft, and most in dreams,
> Ill matching words and deeds long past or late.
> Some such resemblances methinks I find
> Of our last Ev'ning's talk, in this thy dream,
> But with addition strange;
>
> (V, 100–116)

A language which does not refer either to 'external things' or
'deeds long past or late' is a 'mimic Fancy'. The effect of such a
language is to falsify God's creation which, as we learned in
Book VII, is a perfect expression of the Word incarnate.
Opposed to the true image, then, is the simulacrum of the
Satanic creation.

Not only does this opposition distinguish unfallen from fallen
language, but it is also at the root of Milton's general distinction
of the Garden of Eden from other paradisial places in classical
literature:

> Not that fair field
> Of *Enna*, where *Proserpin* gath'ring flow'rs
> Herself a fairer Flow'r by gloomy *Dis*

Was gather'd, which cost *Ceres* all that pain
To seek her through the world; nor that sweet Grove
Of *Daphne* by *Orontes*, and th' inspir'd
Castilian Spring might with this Paradise
Of *Eden* strive;

                                                    (IV, 268–75)

Yet, Milton's Garden depends on all the associations drawn from the classical conceptions of paradise. The difference is that Eden is no single garden, but a synthesis of the most famous in literature. As well, it is the source of all these classical gardens, since what characterizes them is loss, 'which cost *Ceres* all that pain / To seek her through the world'. The 'addition strange' in the classical gardens is 'all that pain' representing the attempt, however fated to misfortune, to retrieve the bliss of paradise. So that in depicting his version of paradise, Milton is conscious of loss, and, for this reason, the description is largely negative.

The literature which attempts to represent paradise is a sequel to the fall. As Edward Said says:

> Words are endless analogies for each other. Outside the monotonous sequence of analogies, we presume, is a primeval Origin, but that, like Paradise, is lost forever. Language is a sequel to or supplement of the beginning event, man's fall: language is one of the events which succeeds the lost Origin. Human discourse, like *Paradise Lost*, lives with the memory of origins long since cut off from it: having begun, discourse can never recover its origins in the unity and unspoken Word of God's Being. This, we know, is the human paradigm incarnated in *Paradise Lost*.[26]

Although Adam can name the animals, this is an unusual event; it is only possible because he is guided by God in an action which is strictly controlled from the outside as God presents the animals in pairs. In addition, Adam is also the product of a prior fall, that of the angels before him in Heaven, and as a result of this, he will have his difficulties with language since, as Raphael says, he is primarily a discursive being:

[26] Said, 'Abecedarium Culturae', p. 35.

the Soul
Reason receives, and reason is her being,
Discursive, or Intuitive; discourse
Is oftest yours, the latter most is ours,
Differing but in degree, of kind the same.

(V, 486–90)

The command of obedience is a godsend, because it is intended
to channel Adam's discursiveness which, before and after the
fall, easily goes astray from word to word in 'wandering mazes
lost'. Obedience is both a check to discursiveness as it is the
'end' toward which his gropings are directed. In addition,
discursiveness and intuition are in 'kind the same', and this
means that the angels and Adam and Eve are intimately
associated in the same problematics of language. For this
reason, we can agree in our analysis with Paul Rozenberg who
argues in a different context that the true bliss of Paradise is
not to be found in Milton's epic, except in a bizarre and distorted fashion: Eve's narcissistic origin which recreates the
bliss found in Heaven before the origin of the disrupting image
and which will be reintroduced anew at the end of time with
'New Heaven, New Earth'.[27]

(iii) Author

Before history, a dialectical and discursive operation (one
should reflect, as well, on the fact that Heaven has a history,
and one in which the Garden of Eden is contained)[28] was the
divine narcissism of self-contemplation, which, we learn in the
discussion between Adam and God in Book VIII, is all the
bliss necessary for God, or, what amounts to the same thing,
before history God's goodness was reflected by the angels in
song and dance. The creation of the Son, and later, of Eden,
cannot add to this beatitude, it can only take away, and, in
keeping with the logic of God's discussion with Adam, it is
God who is most affected by the alteration:

Whereto th'Almighty answer'd, not displeas'd.
A nice and subtle happiness I see

27 'Don, Amour, et Sujétion', *Le Paradi Perdu: 1667–1967*, ed. Jacques
Blondel (Paris: Minard, 1967), pp. 127–9.   28 Rozenberg, pp. 134–5.

> Thou to thyself proposest, in the choice
> Of thy Associates, *Adam*, and wilt taste
> No pleasure, though in pleasure, solitary.
> What think'st thou then of mee, and this my State,
> Seem I to thee sufficiently possest
> Of happiness, or not? who am alone
> From all Eternity. for none I know
> Second to mee or like, equal much less.
> How have I then with whom to hold converse
> Save with the Creatures which I made, and those
> To me inferior, infinite descents
> Beneath what other Creatures are to thee?
>
> (VIII, 398–411)

The passage is fascinating in that the dramatic situation perfectly exemplifies what God is saying, and for this reason,
makes him singularly impressive in a text where everyone has
difficulties in fitting words to events and things. Simply by
speaking to Adam, a 'Creature which I made, and . . . to me
inferior', God undergoes 'infinite descents / Underneath'.[29] Of
great moment in the epic is the fact that it is God who acknowledges his own problematic nature: 'What think'st thou then
of mee?'

This question must be answered, since on the answer depends
Milton's justification of his technique and, as importantly, of
'the ways of God to men'. God is a riddle and a riddler: this is
our first impression and not easily discounted. He enjoys
posing, adopting masks, playing games with Adam, and, in this
attitude, he calls for interpretation and judgement. He fully
intends to give Adam his most 'prized possession', yet requires
that Adam earn this gift. God is not fully trustworthy: he holds
things back, and often means more than he says. Given this
characterization, is it not possible to view the crucial interdiction as but another masking, another riddle which is only so
if one is arrested by its nature as obstacle? Is God's attitude
in his interview with Adam similar to that taken with respect
to the apple?

Our first response is that God's stance is identical in both
cases. As everything is decided beforehand in the discussion of

[29] Rozenberg, p. 129.

a suitable 'helpmate' for Adam, so with the interdiction, as
early as Book III, the outcome of the temptation is predeter-
mined. Why is this so? From the point of view of Milton's
technique, it is obviously a device to frustrate any possibility
of suspense which might accompany the story of the fall, but,
equally, it seems directed at qualifying Raphael's visit and his
lengthy narrative and instruction. Are the middle books of
Paradise Lost to be taken, then, as a form of masking like that
of God in the Garden?

These books represent a partial (in the double sense of
incomplete and slanted) reading of God's ways. Consequently,
the overall impression of God is enigmatic: a creator who, in
the act of creation, causes his own expulsion in creating a
situation where man's victory requires his defeat. It is a matter
of seeing that the creation depends on God's 'retraction'.

> Boundless the Deep, because I am who fill
> Infinitude, nor vacuous the space.
> Though I uncircumscrib'd myself retire,
> And put not forth my goodness, which is free
> To act or not, Necessity and Chance
> Approach not mee, and what I will is Fate.
>
> (VII, 168–73)

Although God does not put forth his 'goodness', the temptation
is to see the creation as good. Following God's own words,
however, we are meant to perceive the creation as equivocal:
neither good nor bad, while potentially it can be either one
or the other, since it is determined by the opposing intentions
of God and Satan. It is the creation itself which poses the
riddle and upon which rests 'justification'.

In this respect, the author of *Paradise Lost* is very much in
God's position as we find him in the invocations seeking his
own justification and creating a problem similar to God's in
statements which can easily be read as retractions. Milton does
not have God's prescience, but he does have his muses, and,
more importantly, he has the finished story of Genesis in hand,
God's own word and the expression of his infinite knowledge.
Like God, Milton's enterprise, then, can only be judged by its
fruits, the goodness which is the final intention of the work

of creation. But this is not necessarily a goodness victorious
over the 'forces of evil', a sham victory over an external
adversary.[30] Rather, it is a goodness which is implicit in the
creation itself, found in the specific reason for the creation:
setting man free.

The earthly creation is, as we know, a compensation for the
loss in Heaven of a third of the angels; more exactly, however,
it is intended to invert the devil's interpretation of the state in
Heaven as bondage into the freedom of the earth. There can
be only one way in Heaven: God's way, which is goodness:

> but the evil soon
> Driv'n back redounded as a flood on those
> From whom it sprung, impossible to mix
> With Blessedness.
>
> (VII, 56–9)

Earth, on the other hand, is a mixed state derived from chaos;
it represents the escape from bondage (for the fallen angels
also) and the perilous acceptance of freedom. As well, it represents an application of the second part of God's definition,
'free to act or not'; from this we are led to his primary nature
as 'good'. Returning to our earlier question ('What think'st
thou of mee?'), the answer need not be equivocal in Milton's
framework; God is goodness and his goodness is exhibited in a
creation where he makes less of himself so that man may be
more, as a free agent who approaches the very nature of the
Godhead. According to this analysis, to be made in the image
of God means not the miming of the attributes of an anthropo-
morphic deity, but to be 'free to act or not'.

In this respect, Satan can be defined as compulsive action
which is based on his idolatrous orientation: his repeated
attempt to physically mirror God in a re-duplication of his
visual attributes—visual components, which are largely of his
own making. Innumerable commentators have noticed that
the effect of this form of imitation is parodic; rather than
taking away from God, on the contrary, it emphasizes the uselessness of such a procedure, and what is useless for Milton is
laughable, as shown in his description of the Paradise of Fools

[30] Fish, *Surprised by Sin*, pp. 179, 192.

or in Samson's characterization of himself as a fool when he laments that he is of no further use to his people.

Stanley Fish emphasizes in his perceptive analysis of the 'War in Heaven', an analysis which focuses on the problematic nature of Abdiel's words and actions, that Milton's concept of true heroism is also grounded on what appears to be useless:

> Abdiel is a hero because he keeps loyalty even when his objective eludes him and his assumptions fail the test of experience. Believing it only just 'That he who in debate of Truth hath won / Should win in Arms,' he does not abandon his post or question the ways of God when his sense of justice is disappointed; and his steadfastness is all the more remarkable because *it is in no sense necessary*. God, Abdiel reminds Satan 'with solitary hand / Reaching beyond all limit, at one blow / Unaided could have finisht thee' (139–41). Or as the poet had written in another place, 'God doth not need / Either man's work or his own gifts.'[31]

Expanding on this theme, Fish ventures a reading of Milton's own biography:

> The desire to serve God is a particularly subtle form of pride if it is in fact a desire to feel needed and important. Milton is especially aware of this danger. In 'When I consider' he murmurs against that decree of God's which has rendered him 'useless' and unable to serve, 'though my Soul more bent / To serve therewith my Maker,' finally admitting 'They also serve who only stand and wait.' The admission, however, is wrung from him with difficulty, and one wonders how long it will be before the passion to be useful reasserts itself. In contrast, Abdiel's acceptance of his uselessness is impressive precisely because it is unconscious. He is able to regard his own superfluousness as a matter of praise and feel no personal injury (sense of injured merit) at all. The perfection of his faith, of his willingness to serve God no matter what service may mean, makes it possible for him to meet unanticipated complications without being demoralized by them. No doubt he is surprised when Satan returns unimpaired,

31 Fish, *Surprised by Sin*, p. 188, emphasis mine.

but surprise is merely wonder (oh, so that's the way it is), not disillusionment; he adjusts to it and goes on.[32]

In the same vein, 'Gabriel *sitting* on a rock in Paradise', or life in Paradise for Adam and Eve 'with the forbidden tree always before them, is such a discipline, calling again for a holding action which is physically unimpressive'.[33] Visually unexciting or 'physically unimpressive', these are the common denominators of true heroic virtue, those 'things invisible to mortal sight' (III, 55), which Milton sets out to depict in *Paradise Lost*.

The charge that the 'War in Heaven' is an exercise in futility can be answered, as Fish does, by showing how futility, the ability to withstand frustration, ridicule, unreasonable demands (the type is Abraham),[34] apparent contradictions, and 'wandering', is the condition of a worthwhile and effective heroism. Like the Garden, the central metaphor of the poem, this attitude appears futile or superfluous, but it is the price of meaning and consistency in *Paradise Lost*.

(iv) Identity and difference

The Adam of *Paradise Lost* and every other character excluding God experience their existence at one time or another in terms of absence, and it is this absence which undercuts the possibility of presence of self and direct and full communication. When a character in the epic believes himself in command and at the centre of things, he is invariably deflated; Abdiel is, of course, the model for this experience. Equally, vindication follows from giving up the claims of self. Dark are the ways of God and darker still are those of man.

Adam is an off-centred creature who destroys the Garden as centre through his fall. The temptation, however, is to transform the centre into a starting point, an origin against which to gauge the 'wandering' of history, especially if history is viewed as the disproportion of word and event through the perspective of Eden. The Garden of Eden is a centre, it is

---

[32] Fish, *Surprised by Sin*, pp. 188–9.
[33] Fish, pp. 195–6.
[34] Fish, p. 200.

believed, because there is found the identity of word and thing, the basis of reliable communication which, in turn, serves to prop up the conception of self as presence. But even in terms of the Garden before the Fall, this strikes us as a false opposition for over and above the Garden is God's providence and 'his prospect high, / Wherein past, present, future he beholds' (III, 77-8). From this perspective, the identity of the Garden is either temporary (at best), or an illusion. (In time, the Garden will become the basic sign of difference as it becomes the metaphor for literary activity, an undertaking which seems radically different from the practical concerns of everyday life. This thesis is underscored by Joseph Summers's recent interpretation of Marvell's 'Garden'.)[35] The only permanent identity in *Paradise Lost* resides, by contrast, with God, the only 'character' those language is perfectly in keeping with the facts.

Adam is an empiricist, and from his empirical standpoint, he does occasionally achieve and experience the identity of word to thing, but he is also a discursive being incapable of comprehending through words the complexities of astronomy in Book VIII. Adam is repeatedly drawn to the visual sense of language and it is this tendency which underlies his conception of language as identity. His experience of Eve, however, alters this conception: she is more than he can say. How are we to situate this contradictory sense of language as expressive of both identity and difference?

The problem is given a particularly lucid formulation by Eugenio Donato:

The relationship that the order of the signifier maintains to the order of the signified, of words to their semantic content, or more simply stated, of words to things, is a paradoxical one, for it is a relationship that has to be defined simultaneously by two propositions which are contradictory: the word *is* the thing; the word is identical to that which it represents, and the space between the two is continuous. Yet words, are different from things, words do not merely represent things; the two orders are discontinuous, their relationship is one of difference.[36]

[35] 'Reading Marvell's "Garden" ', *CR*, XIII (1969), pp. 18-37.
[36] 'The Two Languages of Criticism', p. 94.

This statement has a long history, one which stems most
recently from the French linguist, Saussure, but there is no
need at this point to unravel its complex genealogy. It can be
taken as a starting point and used to show Milton's sense of
language in the central relationship of Adam to Eve as characters and symbolic counters in the play of language.

Although Adam is principally an empiricist who attempts to
found his language on things, he, nevertheless, has a mind,
in the words of *Areopagitica*, 'that can wander beyond all limit
and satiety'.[37] Dissatisfied with his status and with his company
in the Garden when first created, he expresses his desire for a
helpmate, someone made in his *image* with whom he can talk:
'by conversation with his like to help, / Or solace his defects'
(VIII, 418–19). He wants someone different, but not too different; an identical being, yet not himself. God grants his wish:

> Under his forming hands a Creature grew,
> Manlike, but different sex, so lovely fair,
> That what seem'd fair in all the World, seem'd now
> Mean, or in her summ'd up, in her contain'd. . . .
>   (VIII, 470–73)

Eve is the first literary creation: beginning in dreams and
desire and ending as the separate and enclosed entity of Book
IV. Her identity to famous literary types, from Greek myth
to the cruel mistress of Petrarchanism, is the key to our understanding of her role in Milton's epic. Her beauty, the first and
best, exemplifies the aesthetic dimension of the literary work
and it is thoroughly self-sufficient. Adam does violence to her
primary nature when he calls her away from herself in his
desire to subordinate beauty to reason, difference to identity.
What matters for Adam is that she is his 'other self'. She must
be made to conform with his intentions, so he transforms her
beauty into didactic lesson and takes every opportunity to
remind her of her subservience to his 'reason' (merely another
word for Adam's domination of Eve). Yet, she needs no one
else, and only through force can she be redirected to Adam's
ways. Eve, however, will recall her origin with the serpent's
prompting, and will forget her pact with Adam in her desire

[37] Hughes, p. 733.

for independence and equality in order to maintain her difference.

Adam falls in love with his own image, but as an image,
Eve has a life apart. The situation is complex:

> And in her looks, which from that time infus'd
> Sweetness into my heart, unfelt before,
> And into all things from her Air inspir'd
> The spirit of love and amorous delight.
> Shee disappear'd, and left me dark, I wak'd
> To find her, or forever to deplore
> Her loss, and other pleasures all abjure:
> When out of hope, behold her, not far off,
> Such as I saw her in my dream, adorn'd
> With what all the Earth or Heaven could bestow
> To make her amiable:
>
> (VIII, 474–84)

Like a work of art, as Sidney says in the *Defence of Poetry*,
Eve stands for 'amorous delight': she entertains. It remains
for Adam, or, in the case of this passage, it is Raphael's duty
as 'Divine interpreter' (VII, 73) to supply the instruction.
Eve's absence ('shee disappear'd') withdraws a part of Adam:
'which from that time infus'd / Sweetness into my heart, unfelt
before'. While caught up in his divine dream, Adam is no
different from Eve in her narcissistic trance; this is a fullness
and identity which will rarely again be found in a discursive
existence founded on separation and the search to repair the
'loss'. Yet, Eve's beauty, 'the charm of Beauty's powerful
glance' (533), promises a presence and identity which cannot be
re-created by reason and discourse:

> . . . yet when I approach
> Her loveliness, so absolute she seems
> And in herself complete, so well to know
> Her own, that what she wills to do or say,
> Seems wisest, virtuousest, discreetest, best;
> All higher knowledge in her presence falls
> Degraded, Wisdom in discourse with her
> Loses discount'nanc't, and like folly shows;
>
> (VIII, 546–53)

Eve's absoluteness, her beauty, her completeness, in short, her
singular difference always surpasses the manipulations of reason
founded on the piecemeal and successive operations of discourse: 'whereon / In contemplation of created things /
By steps we may ascend to God' (V, 510–12). This gradual and
laborious unfolding of reasonable discourse in a framework of
identity is degraded by the gratification which Eve's beauty,
offers: 'what seem'd fair in all the world, seem'd now / Mean,
or in her summ'd up, in her contain'd'.

In this context, we can appreciate a further theoretical
elaboration supplied by Professor Donato, this time focusing
on the psychoanalytic interpretation of language developed by
Jacques Lacan:

> On the one hand, language is identity based on a system of
> representation that is visual and not linguistic—the word as
> identical to the thing it represents, supported by a visual
> *imago* which constitutes the subject of consciousness. This
> subject implies presence of the self inherited from the
> philosophical tradition that extends from Descartes to
> Merleau-Ponty, but which from Freud on has to be de-
> nounced as illusory, even if this illusion is a necessary in-
> gredient of our everyday life. On the other hand, the subject
> of difference is given to us by language, inasmuch as language
> is difference, a subject that inhabits the order of the signi-
> fier, an off-centered subject which is not present to itself,
> but, is in internal exclusion of itself.[38]

Insofar as Eve is a visual *imago* for Adam, she creates his illusion of presence of self. ((Illusion is exactly Raphael's judgement of Adam's recounting of her creation.) Eve is 'all language',[39] and because of this, she stands for difference, a
difference which causes Adam to forget himself, to be in
'internal exclusion' of himself. In characterizing Eve, Milton
recalls the contradictions of the Narcissus myth, of the relationship of Echo to Narcissus, and he also remembered that self-
contemplation and presence of self is an illusion. (One need

[38] 'The Two Languages of Criticism', p. 95.
[39] Eve may represent, however indirectly, a Miltonic joke (the joke is
on man!) in being a personification of gossip.

not wait for Freud for this recognition.) Particularly, illusion is the punishment for having forsaken the love of Echo.[40] In the sphere of language, the reality is difference and identity is illusory. The question arises: on what ground is language understandable, if its status as thing-oriented is shown to be ultimately involved with a desire for presence, a desire which, in turn, creates the illusion that words are things?

Until man's creation, there appears to be no particular problem; God creates the world in naming it, setting up an original and perfect etymology:

> The Earth obey'd, and straight
> Op'ning her fertile Womb teem'd at a Birth
> Innumerous living Creatures, perfet forms,
> Limb'd and full grown:
>
> . . . the swift Stag from under ground
> Bore up his branching head: scarce from his mould
> *Behemoth* biggest born of Earth upheav'd
> His vastness: Fleec't the Flocks and bleating rose,
> As Plants: ambiguous between Sea and Land
> The River Horse and scaly Crocodile.
>
> . . . First crept
> The Parsimonious Emmet, provident
> Of future, in small room large heart enclos'd,
> Pattern of just equality perhaps
> Hereafter, join'd in her popular Tribes
> Of Commonalty:
>
> (VII, 453–88)

The creation is of 'perfet forms' and words are adequate to their nature; their form expresses their 'end', as in the 'Parsimonious Emmet' or the ambiguity of 'River Horse', since the 'River Horse' resides 'between Sea and Land'. Whether as words or things, the creation is a system of difference, a state of perfect differentiation: even what is ambiguous is only so because of physical placement in a material universe. It is

---

[40] See Jacques Ehrmann, 'The Death of Literature', *NLH*, III (1971), p. 40, for an interesting discussion of literature and its source in echo.

this linguistic and physical hierarchy which, curiously, becomes the source of displeasure for Adam. We know, however,
that it is order at a price: passion has been excluded, that is,
the passions of the fallen angels who had attempted to overturn
a previous hierarchy where, similarly, structure had become
the source of displeasure and contention.[41]

Naturally, with the advent of Adam and Eve, passion will
be reintroduced into the hierarchy and order will be contaminated anew:

> Thus began
> Outrage from lifeless things; but Discord first
> Daughter of Sin, among th' irrational,
> Death introduc'd through fierce antipathy:
> Beast now with Beast gan war, and Fowl with Fowl,
> And Fish with Fish;
>
> (X, 706–11)

The beasts do not initially war with fowl or fish, but among their
own kind, thus destroying from the inside the identity of kind
with kind, and with this destruction, the entire framework is
ruined. These are the obvious fruits of the fall, the deconstruction of language as identity, but the damage is implicit long
before the fall insofar as the narration is by a fallen creature,
who has never possessed the single dispensation of Edenic
innocence. For the narrator, the Garden is an expression of
nostalgia for a perfect origin. Yet, the view is not one-sided,
for balancing the creation of Book VII, in the text, is the 'War
in Heaven' of Book VI, a war fought expressly to determine the
proper interpretation of the word.

(v) Interpretation

The 'War in Heaven' and the Creation are poles between
which our sense of language oscillates, and it is this binary
opposition which is at the centre of our preoccupation with
Paradise Lost. If we seek to establish priority among the two,
we find that chronologically the 'War in Heaven' is first and
that the Son's victory there as *logos* determines the structure of
the creation on earth. The sense of fixity in the Creation, which

[41] Rozenberg, 'Don, Amour, et Sujétion', pp. 130–32.

stems from the identity of words and things, is the result of a successful interpretation (the Son's ability to read the Father's enigmatic words in Book III versus Satan's failure to do so in Book V) which is portrayed in the 'War in Heaven' as the consequence of a simple victory. Although the Son is successful and expels Satan from Heaven, this does not mark the end of the conflict:

> our better part remains
> To work in close design, by fraud or guile
> What force effected not. . . .
>
> But these thoughts
> Full Counsel must mature: Peace is despair'd,
> For who can think Submission? War then, War
> Open or understood, must be resolv'd.
>
> (I, 645–62)

At the end of the poem, Michael, in his prophecy, emphasizes the continuation of the battle:

> Dream not of thir fight,
> As of a Duel, or the local wounds
> Of head or heel: not therefore joins the Son
> Manhood to Godhead, with more strength to foil
> Thy enemy; nor so is overcome
> Satan, whose fall from Heav'n, a deadlier bruise,
> Disabl'd not to give thee thy death's wound:
>
> (XII, 386–92)

The battle continues, since the contending interpretations of the word are endless once words have been wrested from their 'supposed' origin in things.

Having lost their anchoring in things, a disjunction which creates a literal paradise lost, words are free to take on any meaning, and from this stems their ambiguity. Free-floating, words can be used by anyone; they can be manipulated, distorted, and subverted. But since the word no longer has a grounding, since it is caught in a perpetual oscillation of contending polarities, and since the damning accusation in Book XII of *Paradise Lost* concerns the manufacturing of 'carnal words' by the 'grim wolves' who succeed Christ's ministry, what reliable support can words have? What will allow us to believe in them again?

If behind words there is *no-thing*, then the material support of language is nothing else but other words, as what lies behind words is nothing else but other words, and to see nature as an accumulation of words by successive generations is to be caught in the endless jar of interpretation. In this perspective, the narrator of *Paradise Lost* is not merely a scribe being dictated to by Urania. More often, he is an interpreter, a stance which has troubled many critics because they have taken his interpretations as binding on the reader. In addition, everyone else in the poem is an interpreter, from the Son to Raphael, through Satan and Michael, whose task is to transform Adam into an interpreter in Books XI and XII.

Yet, what is there to interpret, if, in the words of Eugenio Donato, 'linguistic signs refer themselves only to other linguistic signs, if the linguistic reference of words is words, if texts refer to nothing but other texts?'[42] In answering this question, Donato sides with Michael Foucault's statement that, 'If interpretation can never accomplish itself, it is simply because there is nothing to interpret.'[43] He continues:

> There is nothing to interpret, for each sign is in itself not the thing that offers itself to interpretation but interpretation of other sings. There is never an *interpretandum* which is not already an *interpretans*, so that a relationship of both violence and elucidation establishes itself with interpretation. Interpretation does not shed light on a matter that asks to be interpreted, that offers itself passively to interpretation, but it can only seize violently an interpretation that is already there, one which it must overturn, overthrow, shatter with the blows of a hammer—the reference here is, of course, to Nietzsche. Interpretation then is nothing but sedimenting one layer of language upon another to produce an illusory depth which gives us the temporary spectacle of things beyond words.[44]

After the Fall, Adam finds himself in a position where he is

---

[42] Donato, 'The Two Languages of Criticism', p. 96.
[43] 'Nietzsche, Marx, Freud', *Cahiers de Royaumont, Philosophie*, 6 (1967), p. 189.   [44] Donato, 'The Two Languages of Criticism', p. 96.

compelled to understand his new status. In death, he discovers, in a word, his 'mortal sentence' (X, 48) behind which there seems to be nothing. Certainly, he observes death among the animals of the Garden—it is this event which leads to his concern—but even as a concrete event, death is meant to be taken as a sign: 'Nature first gave signs' (XI, 182). It is a sign of death because it was first implanted there by Adam's faulty interpretation of Eve, 'his bond of Nature'. Nature, consequently, becomes the sign of his doom, a 'sentence' which is precisely of Adam's own making.

Even before the fall, nature serves the function of interpretation, in that it reflects the status of Adam and Eve in the Garden; specifically, it serves to reveal their privileged status. Satan, aware of this relationship and the way in which they maintain the significant nature of the Garden, forms a part of his temptation of Eve in terms of her position in nature. In this way, he challenges what had earlier been the focus of the discussion by Adam and Raphael of the meaning of the earth as potentially the centre of the universe, as well as the untutored wonder of Adam and Eve over nature's abundance. It is this wonder which causes Eve's separation from Adam to increase their cultivation and control the Garden's abundance. Adam and Eve desire work and the participation in happy labour to the extent that they feel this activity meaningful. Yet, their cultivation makes no mark on the fecundity of the Garden, and it leads to the suspicion that it is useless. In order to see their work as meaningful, they invest nature with a meaning which their labour fails to create. They read into nature their desire to be useful and this interpretation becomes the potential source of confusion as Raphael cautions Adam:

> Solicit not thy thoughts with matters hid,
> Leave them to God above, him serve and fear;
> Of other Creatures, as him pleases best,
> Wherever plac't, let him dispose: joy thou
> In what he gives to thee, this Paradise
> And thy fair *Eve*: Heav'n is for thee too high
> To know what passes there; be lowly wise:
> Think only what concerns thee and thy being;
>
> (VIII, 168–74)

As Raphael sees it, the interpretation of nature, whether on
the cosmic or the local level of the surrounding Garden of
Paradise, is based on the assumption that something lies behind
nature:

> Dream not of other Worlds, what Creatures there
> Live, in what state, condition or degree,
> Contented that thus far hath been reveal'd
> Not of Earth only but of highest Heav'n.
>   (VIII, 175–8)

However comforting Raphael's advice may be, it is, nevertheless, contradictory, for he reveals the secrets of 'other Worlds',
the Heaven upon which this world is founded and in terms of
which nature is meaningful.

Adam has always been uneasy in his world and Raphael does
not resolve his difficulties. Even Raphael's advice to 'joy
thou / In what he gives to thee, this Paradise / And thy fair
Eve' will be retracted when Adam expresses the extent of his
joy in Eve. In order to situate himself more firmly in this world,
Adam interprets his condition as founded on a prior state
which is more stable. But Raphael's narrative of Heaven does
not supply this grounding. On the contrary, it sets him adrift
in a context of contending interpretation where the ultimate
source of meaning is not in things but in the word. This may
serve to give him 'the temporary spectacle of things beyond
words', only, however, as 'an illusory depth'. Adam must learn
to be 'lowly wise' and forsake the 'show of things'.

Returning to Adam's dramatic encounter with death, with
nothing but his 'sentence' in Book X, we discover that the
source of interpretation, that is to say, what lies behind words,
is no more nor less than the person who voices the words and
who gives the interpretation. As Foucault says: 'Interpretation
will henceforth always be an interpretation by the "who". One
does not interpret that which is in a signified but in the last
analysis the one "who" has laid down the interpretation. The
principle of interpretation is nothing but the interpreter
himself.'[45] Adding to this formulation, Donato says, 'What
begins by being the questioning of the subject inevitably turns

[45] Foucault, 'Nietzsche, Marx, Freud', p. 191.

out to be an indictment of him who questions in the first place'.[46]

(vi) The sacrifice of the word

The Son is the first to recognize the 'redounding' nature of interpretation in the circularity of judgement: 'but thou know'st / Whoever judg'd; the worst on mee must light' (X, 72–3). Similarly, Adam says, caught in the throes of his interpretation:

> Him after all Disputes
> Forc't I absolve: all my evasions vain
> And reasonings, though through Mazes, lead me still
> But to my own conviction: first and last
> On mee, mee only, as the source and spring
> Of all corruption, all the blame lights due;
> So might the wrath.
>
> (X, 828–34)

This passage is reminiscent of Satan's words in his soliloquy in Book IV, and, like Satan, Adam continues: 'O Conscience, into what Abyss of fears / And horrors hast thou driven me; out of which / I find no way, from deep to deeper plung'd!' (842–4). Adam is inconsistent, however, as he attempts to fix the blame on Eve:

> nothing wants, but that thy shape,
> Like his, and color Serpentine may show,
> Thy inward fraud, to warn all creatures from thee
> Henceforth; lest that too heav'nly form, pretended
> To hellish falsehood, snare them.
>
> (X, 869–72)

He seeks a scapegoat as the source of his false interpretation, and in his desire to transform Eve to 'color Serpentine', he would change her into a permanent *sign* of falsehood, transform inward to outward shape. The scapegoat seemingly reintroduces proper differentiation in a world sick from the uncertainty of interpretation, the contamination of the world, and the

---

[46] Donato, 'The Two Languages of Criticism', p. 96.

'plague' of Paradise. But, contrary to expectation, the scapegoat feeds Death and propagates further corruption.

This issue of the scapegoat is at the heart of Milton's rejection of censorship in *Areopagitica*, where the expulsion of heretical beliefs, rather than achieving purification, merely creates another obstacle to the eventual victory of truth over falsehood:

> For who knows not that Truth is strong, next to the Almighty. She needs no policies, nor strategems, nor licensings to make her victorious—these are the shifts and the defenses that error uses against her power. Give her but room, and do not bind her when she sleeps, for then she speaks not true, as the old Proteus did, who spake oracles only when he was caught and bound, but then she turns herself into all shapes except her own, and perhaps tunes her voice according to the time, as Micaiah did before Ahab, until she be abjured into her own likeness.[47]

Bound and restricted like a sacrificial victim, truth 'turns herself into all shapes except her own'. Further, the idols are fed innocent blood, and as Milton argues in *Eikonoklastes*, the sacrifice will be revenged on those whose hands are bloodied: 'as the source and spring / Of all corruption, all blame lights due; / So might the wrath'.

In the history of Books XI and XII, truth does not offer the consolation of a glorious victory over the 'forces of evil'. Rather, 'so shall the World go on, / To good malignant, to bad men benign' (XII, 537–8). Truth, in this world, is superfluous, if not, in fact, a source of mockery to those who profess the search for truth, for the ways of the world are to bind truth, to 'tune her voice according to the time'. In history, it is necessary to see truth as different from policy, because a ruling faction is but a more encompassing 'who', a more generalized source of interpretation, which creates the illusion that something lies behind its declarations. The power invested in the state, the power exchanged in a revolution, need not be mysterious insofar as it is the power to punish and create scapegoats. In short, it is the power to make examples, visual illustrations of

[47] Hughes, p. 747.

its word.[48] In the long run, it comes down to the power to validate the law, a law which can itself be appropriated by the more powerful. Thus, it is the one who stands behind or 'outside' the law 'who' is the ultimate source of interpretation. With this observation, we can return to Milton's primary theme in *Paradise Lost*, the justification of the Father as the one who, it is thought, stands outside the law, and, as such, is all-powerful.

The Father creates the Word and, consequently, he is the source of justice. For this reason, it is easy to sympathize with Satan's accusations and his conception of the Father as tyrant. In accusing, however, Satan is no better than the Father, and shortly, we find him setting up his tyranny in Hell. The Father's justice, however, is transferred to the Son, and this action introduces a new element into our understanding of his 'ways'. What this means is that the Father through his image will be made to respond to his own exacting sense of justice. Now inside the law, through his Son, the Father will pay the price of justice which is mercy. This is an exemplary lesson, and it is meant to show that the end of God's justice is self-sacrifice, the willing sacrifice of the Son. Satan, on the other hand, is hypostatized in Book X as 'Rebel to all Law' (83), and this denotes his nature as one who will seek scapegoats in order to satisfy his justice, thus freeing himself to act in the continued belief in his innocence, an innocence which stipulates his exemption from justice and the law.

The sacrifice of others is the Satanic way, and Adam, after the Fall, is all too ready to follow this example (it is his first impulse after he pulls himself together) as he attempts to place the blame on Eve in the judgement of the Son. Adam's speech to the Son reveals the contradictions inherent in the desire for sacrifice:

> O Heav'n! in evil straight this day I stand
> Before my Judge, either to undergo
> Myself the total Crime, or to accuse
> My other self, the partner of my life;
> Whose failing, while her Faith to me remains,
> I should conceal, and not expose to blame

[48] *Cf.* Nietzsche, *The Genealogy of Morals*, First Essay, pp. 460-92.

By my complaint; but strict necessity
Subdues me, and calamitous constraint,
Lest on my head both sin and punishment,
However insupportable, be all
Devolv'd; though should I hold my peace, yet thou
Wouldst easily detect what I conceal.
This Woman whom thou mad'st to be my help,
And gav'st me as thy perfet gift, so good.
So fit, so acceptable, so Divine,
That from her hand I could suspect no ill,
And what she did, whatever in itself,
Her doing seem'd to justify the deed;
Shee gave me of the Tree, and I did eat.

(X, 125–43)

Of note in this passage is that Adam is also accusing God of
sin, since he gave the gift 'so good / So fit, so acceptable, so
Divine'. The accusation leads to a counter-accusation: 'Was
she thy God, that her thou didst obey / Before his voice?'
(145–6). There would be no end to accusations were it not
for the Son, the one who puts an end to the accusations of
justice through his mercy, who cuts off the debate and brings
Adam to justice 'without delay / to Judgment he proceeded '
(163–4). This part of the Son's action is followed by:

then pitying how they stood
Before him naked to the air, that now
Must suffer change, disdain'd not to begin
Thenceforth the form of servant to assume,
As when he wash'd his servants' feet

(X, 211–15)

Justice interpreted by mercy spells the end of interpretation,
of accusation, of scapegoats, and external sacrifice. Coming in
the shape of a master, the Son departs in the form of servant,
as in the New Testament he comes to do the Father's work.

Similarly, Milton wrote of Christ in the divorce tracts; he is
found 'not so much interpreting the Law with his words, as
referring to his own words to be interpreted by the Law'.[49] The

49 Cited by Fish, *Surprised by Sin*, p. 21.

law is not abrogated by the Son, it is not interpreted, but, on the contrary, the Son's words are themselves to be interpreted by the law, and in this sense he will fulfil it to the letter. The law is no obstacle for the Son, because, in the example of his understanding of the Father's words in Book III, it is seen as an opening, specifically, an invitation to service as servant to the Lord. 'I come to do my Father's bidding.'

With the judgement, Adam is 'brought down / To dwell on even ground with (his) Sons' (XI, 347–8). No privileged status any longer for the Father; no one beyond the law, but a community of Sons responsive to an internalized word. This spells the end of mystification and of an interpretation of the Father as source of rivalry. We are not asked to be like the Father; this is impossible. Rather, the model is the Son. He is the image which spells the end of imitation, in sacrificing himself as a god so that man might live. In giving up interpretation, Adam is asked to forsake his propensity for accusation, the method by which he transforms himself into a god in the sacrifice of Eve. Realizing that there is nothing to interpret, unless to determine his own damnation, he learns to live by faith. Consequently, he is asked to substitute for suspicion, trust, and for domination, the free exercise of reason in acknowledging 'that suffering for Truth's sake / Is fortitude to highest victory, / And to the faithful Death the Gate of Life' (XII, 569–71). Man creates his own obstacles, and it is a man, a man descended from Godhead, who shows that obstacles are not final since they are man-made. And it is to these obstacles that the iconoclastic temper of *Paradise Lost* is directed, so that by the end of the poem, there is *no-thing* left but 'thir solitary way'.

6
The 'Master work':
the folding structure of
Paradise Lost

> For Heav'n
> Is as the Book of God before thee set,
> Wherein to read his wond'rous Works, and learn
> His Seasons, Hours, or Days, or Months, or Years:
>
> (VIII, 66–9)

> That day, as other solemn days, they spent
> In song and dance about the sacred Hill,
> Mystical dance, which yonder starry Sphere
> Of Planets and of fixt in all her Wheels
> Resembles nearest, mazes intricate,
> Eccentric, intervolv'd, yet regular
> Then most, when irregular they seem:
>
> (V, 618–24)

> If an eternal traveller were to cross it in any direction, after
> centuries he would see that the same volumes were repeated
> in the same disorder (which, thus repeated, would be an
> order: the Order). My solitude is gladdened by this elegant
> hope.
>
> Borges, 'The Library of Babel'

(i) Chaos within bounds

An erroneous impression may have been given in the last
chapter that *Paradise Lost*, in being an indictment of iconic
representations in art, stands more generally for a condemnation
of art. In addition, the argument that the function of inter-

pretation is at the heart of Milton's conception of the sign might have created the assumption that this delimits the possibility of any other understanding of his use of language in *Paradise Lost*. Certainly, the alternative to interpretation is not visual representation (again, the distinction between the false alternatives of criticism and literature), since this is to be involved in the bondage of self-fulfilling desires which merely enhance an illusory 'presence of self'.

In the last section, the approach to the theme of justification in *Paradise Lost* was to show that in his 'retraction' God desires only good for man, so much so that he sacrifices himself in the form of his 'resplendant image' so that man can be free. But *Paradise Lost* is equally a hymn of praise and a monument of wonder over the resplendent nature of God's ways, and, in this sense, it is like the 'morning prayer' of Adam and Eve in Book V.[1] Where the initial form of justification depended on a process of deconstruction, the sense we wish to develop presently will require, by contrast, seeing the poem in the large. For it is the overview which gives us the unifying and integral sense of God's ways and which the narrator rises to in Book III. Thus, rather than oppositions, contention, polarities, and the endless process of interpretation, we will find unity, proportion and coherence; this time, however, not at God's expense, but at our own. His greatness, his infinity, his wondrous ways will serve to delimit us in highlighting the reader's finite stature: 'May I express thee unblam'd?' (III, 3).

Even though the poem expresses a magnitude which belittles the reader, it is, nevertheless, true that out of finitude is created a hymn fully expressive of the infinity of God. The infinity of God is, from one point of view, inexpressible and mysterious. However, this is not the aspect which Milton will emphasize, because the mysterious and the mystifying are the devices of a corrupting clergy whose fundamental aim is enslavement. Under the banner of mystery, they condemn heresies, limit the free investigation of truth, and secure their power as the secret revelation of God to the chosen few. Mystery, in this

---

[1] See Joseph Summers, *The Muses Method* (London: Chatto & Windus, 1962), esp. Chapter III, pp. 71–86; and Michael Fixler, 'The Apocalypse within *Paradise Lost*', *New Essays on Paradise Lost*, ed. Thomas Kranidas (Berkeley: University of California Press, 1969), pp. 131–2.

sense, is the unthinkable and the irrational and contradicts
Milton's belief in revelation; everything necessary to salvation
has been given by God in his written Word. The truth of
scriptures, in the relationship of type to anti-type, concerns the
destruction and elimination of the 'veil' of secrecy in an open
temple to which all are welcomed.

Infinity is, consequently, infinity within bounds, not endless
succession in time, but propagation within the limits of a finite
series, within the bounds of male and female which produce
'multitudes':

> and other Suns perhaps
> With thir attendant Moons thou wilt descry
> Communicating Male and Female Light,
> Which two great Sexes animate the World,
> Stor'd in each Orb perhaps with some that live.
> For such vast room in Nature unpossest
> By living Soul, desert and desolate,
> Only to shine, yet scarce to contribute
> Each Orb a glimpse of Light, convey'd so far
> Down to this habitable, which returns
> Light back to them, is obvious to dispute.
>   (VIII, 148–58)

It is a spatial, not a temporal, infinity on which 'communication'
is based. The spatial hierarchy of the Garden is also a form of
communication; the keeping of place is a sign of obedience
which guarantees a continued conversation with the angels
and God, while disobedience, the breaking of the hierarchy,
signifies the end of communication: 'Now therefore bend thine
ear / To supplication, hear his sighs though mute; / Unskilful
with what words to pray, . . .' (XI, 30–31). Out of the essential
difference of things and words, a difference which is posited
on a spatial model, is created the infinite variety of creation, and
correspondingly, the reflective prayer of Adam and Eve:

> Lowly they bow'd adoring, and began
> Thir Orisons, each Morning duly paid
> In various style, for neither various style
> Nor holy rapture wanted they to praise

> Thir Maker, in fit strains pronounct or sung
> Unmeditated, such prompt eloquence
> Flow'd from thir lips, in Prose or numerous Verse,
>
> (V, 144–50)

Adam and Eve give voice to the order of creation as later, in a contrasting passage (the organization of the poem will be discussed in the next pages),[2] the creation as depicted in the discussion of astronomy 'voices' their status and happiness.

The end of creation is communication, the communication of God's goodness and bounty and the reciprocal action of the created mirroring God's love in adoration and prayer. As Satan recognizes:

> Forgetful what from him I still receiv'd,
> And understood not that a grateful mind
> By owing owes not, but still pays, at once
> Indebted and discharg'd; what burden then?
>
> (IV, 54–7)

So it was in Heaven, and on earth the plan is recreated:

> There wanted yet the Master work, the end
> Of all yet done; a Creature who not prone
> And Brute as other Creatures, but endu'd
> With Sanctity of Reason, might erect
> His Stature, and upright with Front serene
> Govern the rest, self-knowing, and from thence
> Magnanimous to *correspond* with Heav'n,
> But grateful to acknowledge whence his good
> Descends, thither with heart and voice and eyes
> Directed in Devotion, to adore
> And worship God Supreme who made him chief
> Of all his works:
>
> (VII, 505–16, my italics)

Knowing God aright is devotion, adoration, prayer, or 'so it had been'. From an original difference, God / angels, God / man, arises the endless procreation of song and dance, an

2 See below, p. 111, for a diagram of the poem's structure.

infinity within bounds which moves from the highest to the lowest.

The impression, however, is chaotic: 'Prose or numerous Verse', rapture or dance 'yet regular / Then most, when most irregular they seem'. We, perhaps, long for the symmetrical marching files of the rebel angels in Hell, for the logical progression of Satan's journey to earth, for the retributive righteousness of the history in Books XI and XII. Yet the comparison of order and disorder is informative: the order of Heaven seems disordered from the earth, and earthly order is disorder for Heaven, and this because the *end* is different. The proper end of the creation is correspondence and communication in the exercise of free reason, which is love given and repaid, while communication on earth comes to be seen as persuasion, in the domination of another through the sophistic use of language. This represents order but at the price of 'variety' and free inquiry.[3]

As we know, the passage from Heaven to earth is a narrowing (to this 'pinfold') as the narrator says: 'Half remains unsung, but narrower bound / Within the visible Diurnal Sphere' (VII, 21–2). This movement represents a curtailing of the multiple associations which have been built up in the first six books of the epic into the 'strict necessity' of the Fall, and with this confinement of the theme, there would seem to be an attendant shift in the capability of language to reflect adoration and unmediated prayer. With this shift, we locate order in necessity—an order, however, which is the product of an internal disorder, exactly the opposite of what we found in Heaven where external disorder stood for internal order.

Nevertheless, the sense of chaos remains, and this impression is fed by the knowledge that the dance of adoration is without a centre. This is less true of Heaven than of the creation on earth, however, for, in Heaven, the angels do dance around the mount of God, while on earth, the dance of the planets and stars, and for that matter, the adoration of Adam and Eve, is founded on the absence of a centre, an absence which causes both the rapture of Heaven and the unceasing abundance of nature in the Garden.

[3] Claude Lévi-Strauss, *Tristes Tropiques* (New York: Atheneum Press, 1967), p. 397. Lévi-Strauss argues that communication depends on multiple levels of reference.

Communication, then, is the product of an absence at the centre, of a rupture and disruption which follows the creation of the Son as image and *logos*. With the creation and the rebellion of Satan and his crew, God is drawn into the oscillating dance of 'contraries', and, as Jacques Derrida writes in a different context:

> This moment was that in which language invaded the universal problematic; that in which, in the absence of a center or origin, everything became discourse—provided we can agree on this word—that is to say, when everything became a system where the central signified, the original or transcendental signified, is never absolutely present outside a system of differences. The absence of the transcendental signified extends the domain and the interplay of signification *ad infinitum.*[4]

If we seek the actual origin of *Paradise Lost*, in terms of our reading experience, we find it in Hell in Book I; if we seek 'presence of self', we see it in Satan ('Which way I fly is Hell; myself am Hell' [IV, 75]); if we seek work, seriousness, purpose, in short, all human values which are based on the nobility of self, we find it in Hell. These values will, of course, be transferred to earth after the Fall. Heaven and paradise, on the other hand, are havens for play, dance, and song, and the work there, we need to be reminded, is the joyful work of cultivation. In the same vein, the activity of the angels guarding Eden from Satanic invasion is made up largely of angelic games.

Not surprisingly, after the Fall, play becomes suspect:

> Here Love his golden shafts imploys, here lights
> His constant Lamp, and waves his purple wings,
> Reigns here and revels; not in the bought smile
> Of Harlots, loveless, joyless, uninder'd,
> Casual fruition, nor in Court Amours,
> Mixt Dance, or wanton Mask, or Midnight Ball,
> Or Serenate, which the starv'd Lover sings
> To his proud fair, best quitted with disdain.
>
> (IV, 763-70)

---

[4] 'Structure, Sign, and Play', in *The Languages of Criticism*, p. 249.

'Casual fruition' and 'starv'd Lover', products of the Fall, replace the joyful union of Paradise, a playing which, though apparently without purpose, is directed to the *end* of adoration, the function of the 'Master work'. In a more immediate sense, the love of Adam and Eve will lead to the concrete 'fruition' of offspring which, if all went well, would be a sign of further devotion to God. So that in play and interplay, man communicates with God, communicates through his natural motions his joy in the creation and in its abundance.

More specifically, in terms of Derrida's statement, the creation in Book VII is described as the result of God's absence (his 'retraction'), not, however, because he becomes a *deus absconditus* withdrawing from the creation. Rather, he is absent as centre insofar as his effective might is taken over by the Son who involves himself in the creation as present inside 'a system of differences'. Although in the material creation of Book VII this involvement seems a transcendent operation, as reported by Raphael, we learn through Adam's account of his origin in Book VIII that the Son's action in the creation represents an entry into the system, as later, in the prophecy of Michael, he enters history to become the 'one greater Man' of the first invocation. And what denotes the Son's participation in the creation is discourse with Adam, where 'the original or transcendental signified is never absolutely present outside a system of differences'.

This is particularly interesting in terms of Milton's epic intentions, that is to say, of his keeping to the epic requirement of encyclopedic comprehension. Next in importance to the portrayal of heroic demeanor, the epic form was traditionally understood to be a total representation of a given culture; as epic, it contains everything a culture values, and it is because of this that the epic requires on the part of the poet a long and arduous apprenticeship: 'Since first this Subject for Heroic Song / Pleas'd me long choosing, and beginning late' (IX, 25–6). Yet, as Milton overturns the heroic pretensions of the epic, so he reinterprets its 'totalizing' intentions. Rejecting the accumulated knowledge of culture (as we see in the Christ of *Paradise Regained*), and the attempts of finite man to comprehend the limitless scope of God's creation, he develops the far more approachable role of 'lowly wise'.

The absence of God as centre, that is, his inclusion through the Son in the discourse of the creation, accomplishes what could not be done in any other way. In terms of Milton's central preoccupation with a lost condition, the representation of abundance is depicted as the consequence of a finite lack, in the inclusion of the 'central signified' in the play of the signifier. For this reason, the creation is too much; more than one can *say*. The act of cultivation in the Garden stands for the attempt to order the superfluity of signification in the same way that Adam's concern over astronomy represents his attempt to 'make sense' of things. Following this analysis, we can appreciate the extent to which earth is a by-product and a continuing reflection of Chaos.

> On heav'nly ground they stood, and from the shore
> They view'd the vast immeasurable Abyss
> Outrageous as a Sea, dark, wasteful, wild,
> Up from the bottom turn'd by furious winds
> And surging waves, as Mountains to assault
> Heav'n's highth, and with the Centre mix the Pole.
>
> (VII, 210–15)

The earthly creation does represent the mixing of the centre with the pole, but this need not be read as an indictment of the creation. On the contrary, the creation is the raising of Chaos to the level of order, the *order*, which becomes 'matter' for further praise of the Creator. With the creation, Chaos is no longer a separate domain, but 'circumscribed' by the power of the Son, by 'the dear might of him who walked the waves'. Chaos, no longer an obstacle to faith, becomes a further confirmation of the 'ways of God to man'. This must be understood, however, in the precise sense in which the ordering takes place:

> and in his hand
> He took the golden Compasses, prepar'd
> In God's Eternal store, to circumscribe
> This Universe, and all created things:
>
> (VII, 225–7)

The circle, symbol of eternity and order, records the nature of prayer, dance, and adoration: the order of disorder. It

stands for the mirrored structure of the universe, and it is, at
once, movement and static wonder, so that all created things
(this, of course, includes the Son), whether they want to or not
(the potential source of disorder), are bound by the providence
of God and reflect his 'mysterious' ways:

> Yet doubt not but in Valley and in Plain
> God is as here, and will be found alike
> Present, and of his presence many a sign
> Still following thee, still compassing thee round
> With goodness and paternal Love, his Face
> Express, and of his steps the track Divine.
>
> (XI, 349–54)

The 'golden Compasses' will 'still (compass) thee round'. Chaos
transformed by the creation, disorder as order, and *concordia
discord*, this is Milton's view of the circle of perfection and God's
providence.

(ii) Two voices

Read from beginning to end, *Paradise Lost* is particularly disturbing; we can appreciate the metaphoric sense of the blind
poet invoked at the beginning of Books VII and IX, feeling
his way in the dark, much as Adam, in the long interlude of the
middle books, must find his way with Raphael. Numerous
false starts, hesitations, and interruptions are balanced by
presumptions, faulty identifications, accusations, and counter-
accusations: beginning nowhere and leading 'God knows where'.
Milton acknowledges in the statement on the verse which he
appended to the second edition of the poem that there is no
rhyme in the poem, but a firmly held conviction on first reading
the poem might well be: 'No rhyme or reason'.[5] What are we
to make, then, of an apparent 'technique of failure', where we
are shown something only to have it taken away, where the
most stunning passages of the poem are subsequently dis-
credited, where we are repeatedly told by the narrator that
he finds it impossible to say what he would like to, and, where.
finally, we are told that the whole enterprise may be fated

[5] T. S. Eliot, 'Milton (1947)', in Thorpe, pp. 310–32.

to oblivion: 'an age too late, or cold / Climate, or Years damp my intended wing / Deprest' (IX, 44–6)?

The difficulty is eliminated, once we realize that *Paradise Lost* is, in fact, two poems: one written by the narrator and the other by Milton's muse, as we see in the continuation of the passages quoted above: 'and much they may, if all be mine, / Not Hers who brings it nightly to my Ear' (46–7). The narrator's poem is written in time; it is successive, linear, tedious, and doomed to failure. On the other hand, Milton, under the guise of Urania, recreates the circularity and pefection of the creation:

> Descend from Heav'n *Urania*, by that name
> If rightly thou art call'd, whose Voice divine
> Following, above th' *Olympian* Hill I soar,
> Above the flight of *Pegasean* wing.
> The meaning, not the Name I call: for thou
> Nor of the Muses nine, nor on the top
> Of old *Olympus* dwell'st, but Heav'nly born,
> Before the Hills appear'd, or Fountain flow'd,
> Thou with Eternal Wisdom didst converse,
> Wisdom thy Sister, and with her didst play
> In presence of th' Almighty Father, pleas'd
> With thy Celestial Song.
>
> (VII, 1–12)

'Converse' and 'play', key words in our analysis, stand out in this passage; behind 'names' and 'flight', and 'before the Hills appear'd, or Fountain flow'd' stands a conversation which is play and from which stems all words and things and the possibility of words as things. In calling for the meaning, not the name, Milton emphasizes the constructive quality of 'play' which, apparently purposeless, nevertheless, pleases God.

The conscious narrator, who attempts his justification through the device of classification and naming, will come to nought, but this role is countered by the playful muse creating meaning at the expense of the speaker: 'More safe I sing with mortal voice, unchang'd / To hoarse or mute, though fall'n on evil days, / On evil days though fall'n, on evil tongues' (24–6). Consequently, if the speaker depends solely on himself, his 'evil days' will be read as the expression of 'evil tongues', a reminder of the confusion of tongues in Babel and an expression of disorder. Thus it is to equate meaning and name, since names after the fall represent man's internal disorder. So the invocation requests the innocent play before the fall which founds meaning, not as an end in itself, but as the grounding of conversation whose intent is to please God, and, in this way, it introduces order to daily devotion. The troubled conscience of the narrator is an obstacle to faith, if faith is recognized as an invitation to the 'feast of the Lord' as we saw in 'Lycidas'. Order, in *Paradise Lost*, does not stem from the narrator's stricken conscience, but from the 'inspiration' of the muses in conversation with God as a sort of oblique counter-point to the sequential action of the poem. For this reason, the order of the poem will appear accidental (the operation of grace) as it evolves from disorder.

The diagram on p.111 has been included to illustrate the nature of this relationship as it is reflected in the structure of the poem. This structure is far different from that which has been argued by Arthur Barker and, in a more recent essay, by John Shawcross.[6] The emphasis of both Barker and Shawcross is on the redistribution of the ten books of the first edition of *Paradise Lost* into twelve when the epic was re-issued in 1674. The difference between Barker and Shawcross is that the former prefers the second version insofar as the change 'reduce(s) the structural emphasis on the Fall of man and . . . increase(s) the emphasis on his restoration'.[7] Without going into particulars, Shawcross argues for the first edition order of the books, because it gives a firmer outline to the action. Unlike Barker, whose argument is based on the dramatic form of the epic, Shawcross reveals that *Paradise Lost* has a duplicating structure, in that the original first five books are a model for the action in the last five (in the second edition, the last six books are contrasted to the first six), so that we find the order as shown at the top of p.112 (first edition):

[6] Arthur Barker, 'Structural Pattern in *Paradise Lost*', in *Milton: Modern Essays in Criticism*, pp. 142–55; John T. Shawcross, 'The Balanced Structure of *Paradise Lost*', *SP*, LXII (1965), pp. 696–718.
[7] Barker, 'Structural Pattern in *Paradise Lost*', pp. 146–7.

DUPLICATING STRUCTURE*

	(A)	(B)	(C)	(D)
I	Solitary;	Idol-unity;	Pandemonium	
II	Council;	Past = Sin + Death, Gates of Hell;	Chaos;	New World
III	Heaven;	Son's mercy;	Limbo of vanity;	Mt. Niphates
IV	Satan's soliloquy;	Eden, Adam and Eve, and debate;	Dream;	Scales
V	Eve's dream interpreted;	Morning prayer;	Raphael descends;	History of Satan
VI	Warning angels;	Difference to identity;		Son as image
VII	Warring atoms;	Difference to identity;		Man as image
VIII	Astronomy interpreted;	History of Adam;		Raphael descends
IX	Satan's soliloquy;	Adam and Eve debate;	Fall;	Endless argument
X	Heaven;	Son's judgement;	Bridge over Chaos;	Repentance of Adam and Eve and Narrator
XI	Council;	Past = Sin + Death on earth;	Flood;	New World
XII	Babel;	Idol-disunity;	Solitary	

INVOCATIONS

* There are a number of inconsistencies in this chart; Books I and XII are reversed books, while all the other pairings represent corresponding sequential patterns, a parallel development from A to D, with reversals attuned to individual sections. For instance, IIIB is the obverse of XB. Moreover, the determination of individual sections is somewhat arbitrary: the separation of individual units (A, B, C, D) is not as distinct or inevitable as one might wish it to be. The labels serve an interpretative function and propose an analytic sense of a given passage. As interpretation, there is room for debate. Nevertheless, the diagram is not incoherent to the extent that it records the labyrinthian organization of the epic. The rationale for this organization can be argued in a context similar to that advanced by Michael Fixler in "The Ap[...], see pp. [...]

I   : VI
II   : VII
III : VIII
IV   : IX
V   : X

The effect of this organization, Shawcross says, is contrast
in order to drive home the lessons of 'justification'.[8] It is an
attractive theory, and there is no question that Shawcross is
correct in his description. Our objection, however, is that
Paradise Lost is not only a book intended to be read from
beginning to end: a poem which begins by portraying the ways
of other worlds in order to set up a rationale for subsequent
action on earth. This procedure is far too 'rational' and didactic,
qualities we come to suspect as a mask for an a priori righteousness—the very form of self-fulfilment practised by Satan who
sets up hypothetical problems only to show that he can solve
them, thus securing his position. As this method creates a false
security for Satan, so it functions for the narrator, who becomes
increasingly uncomfortable as the poem progresses and his
hypothetical scheme backfires: Christ wins in Heaven at the
end of the first six books, but man loses on earth, or so it seems.

Looked at differently, the narrator's problem is the result of
his fundamental identification with Satan, that is to say, that
what he describes in the poem is the Odyssean voyage of Satan
from his world to ours in an ironic interpretation of the Homeric
and Virgilian theme of 'homecoming'. Satan returns home in
Book X after a successful journey, after having transformed
earth into a mirror of Hell, a process which will be played out
in full in Michael's history of the earth. So that a sequential
reading of the poem, interrupted by numerous interludes, is, in
fact, not a hymn of adoration in a conversation which mirrors
the providence of God. Rather, it is the enacting of the speech
of damnation; it is invective and curse in a mirroring of the
Satanic enterprise. Correspondingly, the hymn of the earth is
the cursing and rejecting of God's ways: it is, in a word, the
fall into damnation.

Importantly, there is another mirror in the Son, who is
found in the gap separating Books VI and VII and what it

[8] Shawcross, 'The Balanced Structure of *Paradise Lost*', p. 711.

shows is that Satan and man fulfil God's words even when they are unaware that they are doing so. It is a mirror in which disorder is order: man's disorder inverted in the mirror of the Son is God's order, the order of the muse who 'plays' in his presence. In this context, what we discover as the muses' structure in the poem (as our diagram shows) is the disordered movement from Book I to VI, which is then repeated, only this time in reverse:

$$
\begin{array}{l}
\text{I} \quad : \text{XII} \\
\text{II} \quad : \text{XI} \\
\text{III} : \text{X} \\
\text{IV} : \text{IX} \\
\text{V} \quad : \text{VIII} \\
\text{VI} : \text{VII}
\end{array}
$$

The poem requires a simultaneous reading from the beginning and from the end, for Book I begins where Book XII ends, in the solitariness of the speaker, his own 'temple', like the solitude of Satan awaking on the burning lake, trying to find his way. Satan's stance as solitary is also repeated by Adam and Eve who 'with wandering steps and slow' find 'thir solitary way'. So the end of VI connects with the beginning of VII, as XII joins with I.

The model is the circle, which is connected at two crucial points, the first and the seventh invocations. The poem as worship, as vocal prayer, is a plea to God and through the mediation of the Son, it is heard and returned to man as mercy shown:

What better can we do, than to the place
Repairing where he judg'd us, prostrate fall
Before him reverent, and there confess
Humbly our faults, and pardon beg, with tears
Watering the ground, and with our sighs the Air
Frequenting, sent from hearts contrite, in sign
Of sorrow unfeign'd, and humiliation meek.
Undoubtedly he will relent and turn
From his displeasure; in whose look serene,
When angry most he seem'd and most severe,

What else but favor, grace, and mercy shone?
  So spake our Father penitent, nor *Eve*
Felt less remorse: they forthwith to the place
Repairing where he judg'd them prostrate fell
Before him reverent, and both confess'd
Humbly thir faults, and pardon begg'd, with tears
Watering the ground, and with thir sighs the Air
Frequenting, sent from hearts contrite, in sign
Of sorrow unfeign'd, and humiliation meek.

                      (X, 1086–104)

The narrator can repeat 'our Father penitent' in the same spirit that the Son, in Book III (the Book which is the reverse of X in the mirrored structure) repeats the Father in humility. From the narrator's point of view, there is no more to say, as action accords with word; he also has returned to that 'place', has humbled himself, and has, therefore, reversed God's anger to 'favour, grace, and mercy shone'.

  What appears as a 'wandering way', the labyrinth of interpretation and false steps, is transformed into 'unmediated strains' which mirror the glory and goodness of God's ways to man. What seemed 'most irregular' is shown, finally, to be 'yet regular', and as Borges writes in 'The Library of Babel', a story which strikes us as having been composed with *Paradise Lost* in mind: 'My solitude is gladdened by this elegant hope.'[9]

[9] *Labyrinths* (New York: New Directions, 1962), p. 58.

7
Human ways:
violence and its discontent

The last thing *I* should promise would be to 'improve' mankind. No new idols are erected by me; let the old ones learn what feet of clay mean. *Overthrowing idols* (my word for 'ideals')—that comes closer to being part of my craft. One has deprived reality of its value, its meaning, its truthfulness, to precisely the extent to which one has mendaciously invented an ideal world.

Nietzsche, *Ecce Homo*

(i) 'Seeming pure'

The 'inspiration' of the 'Master work' balances the deadening reality of deconstruction and interpretation, and both are singularly human processes. The symmetry and reciprocity implicit in Milton's circular poem may be ascribed to Urania, but, of course, it is Milton who wrote the poem and fully intended its apparent contradictions, founded as they are on the paradoxical nature of language. Insofar as the poem is a description of things, it fails miserably to record the benevolent ways of God to man; rather, in this context, *Paradise Lost* is substantially an illustration of doom. On the other hand, as the poem is the recording of a long and arduous penitence, or an extended flight above things—in this sense, it is a free expression of the 'Spirit'—Milton can accomplish his intention in praising the ways of God to man. Thus, *Paradise Lost* gives hope as a language founded, not on the identity of word and things, but on difference. And, at least initially, it is this conception of language as difference which does violence to our desires and expectations.

In terms of the dramatic context of the poem, it is a matter of the Son as true image destroying Satan as simulacrum, as Satan attempts to found his empire on earth and on things.

This intention gives way to the unexpected—there is nothing in nature which would lead us to expect it—and divine intercession of the Word as pure difference from the failing ways of man and Satan.

What has been described as the contradictory nature of language can be seen in a more immediate and passionate perspective once we seize on the fact that this contradiction is the violence one charaterization of language does to another; the interplay of the two senses of language is nothing but the physical displacement of Satan by God's wrath. But over and above this relationship of violence, the hammering out of new interpretations from the ruin of older ones, is the relationship of elucidation in the repetition of the same mistake through history, elucidation depending on the perception that mistakes in history are always the same as that of our 'original parents'. There may be variants on the original Fall, but the variants simply validate the norm.[1] As violence becomes associated with man's ways in *Paradise Lost*, and, as it is shown to be, at base, a method of self-deception, so the poem is directed to a 'revelation' and elucidation of the dark ways of man.

What makes *Paradise Lost* impressive is its emphasis that salvation is the product of man as he is found in the world; Christ does not save an ideal conception of man, but, as was said above,[2] he shows the ways of salvation to Adam, the model of a vain, redundant, and petty creature. Specifically, Christ saves man in 'humiliation meek'. Consequently, it is Adam's mistakes which save him as long as he can recognize them as personal lapses, as it is out of an actual human reality in all its banality that Milton constructs the ladder which leads to Heaven, illustrated in Book V by the redemptive image of the tree:

> So from the root
> Springs lighter the green stalk, from thence the leaves
> More aery, last the bright consumate flow'r
> Spirits odorous breathes: (479–82)

---

[1] *Cf.* Ehrmann, 'The Death of Literature', p. 38. 'If a variance exists—and we are convinced that it does—it is not a variance *in relation* to a norm, but rather a variance *within* the norm. Or, more precisely, the norm (the law of language) is founded on the possibility of variance.'

[2] See p. 65.

The root is in the earth out of which man springs, a talking beast to be lamented as much for his talk as for his beastliness. The earth is the sign of Satan's reign in this world as it is the 'end' of human pretensions turned into 'dust'; it is also, however, the sign of Satan's downfall:

> Because thou hast done this, thou art accurst
> Above all Cattle, each Beast of the Field;
> Upon thy Belly groveling thou shalt go,
> And dust shalt eat all the days of thy Life.
> Between Thee and the Woman I will put
> Enmity, and between thine and her Seed;
> Her Seed shall bruise thy head, thou bruise his heel.
>
> (X, 175–81)

The seed, the 'greater Man' of the poem's opening, will grow from a weak thing to subvert Satanic strength.[3] The method of this victory, however, is not mysterious; neither is it in any obvious sense heroic. It comprehends all knowledge and wisdom but is known by simple words:

> only add
> Deeds to thy knowledge answerable, add Faith,
> Add Virtue, Patience, Temperance, add Love,
> By name to come call'd Charity, the soul
> Of all the rest:
>
> (XII, 581–5)

Thus, Milton develops an 'ideal' which contradicts the traditional conception of idealism. So that what is being delineated in *Paradise Lost* is not the ideal sweep and comprehension of an epic narrative; nor is it an ideal characterization of man always in control of his destiny who, because he thinks himself in the 'right', can vanquish his adversary; nor is the promised end in any recognizable sense ideal, except as it lies in a distant, if not infinite, future which will be ushered in by God, without man's help. In the light of this, the only level of comprehension is a sluggish and uncompromising reality.

[3] See also XII, 566–73.

But here, especially, we need to be wary of the word, reality, lest we transform it into but another mirror of an ideal conception. On the contrary, the nature of reality in *Paradise Lost* is all too recognizable in Abdiel's or Adam's misconceptions and weaknesses which are summed up in the 'wandering' ways of history. History is the final temptation in that it presents itself as a series of actions directed to a goal, an ideal which will recuperate its labyrinthine course. The truth of Christ's apparition in history, for instance, was understood in terms of a Messianic promise. But this truth is incomplete unless its problematic nature is grasped: he came only to disappear again. As Oscar Cullman writes in *Christ and Time*, in the prophetic and apocalyptic books of the Old Testament, the Messiah was expected to introduce the end of the line of history, and when Christ's promise failed to materialize in an apocalyptic judgement, the early Christians were forced to reinterpret Christ's ministry as a middle, not as ending.[4] This analysis is reminiscent of Milton's statements in *Areopagitica*, concerning the temporary apparition of the 'glorious shape of truth' which came into the world only to disappear.

History does contain the ideal, but it is an ideal which must be counterbalanced by its 'wandering' ways, or, more exactly, the ideal can only be perceived through 'wandering' ways, not, however, as an alternative—a 'leap of faith'—but as intermingled with the concrete and material events of history. History, as the 'mangled body of truth', is, nevertheless, *the truth* of man's existence.

In *Paradise Lost*, we find this explicit reading in the last two books, yet it is metaphorically present much earlier in the Garden of Eden, which contains 'in narrow room Nature's whole wealth' (IV, 207), The Garden does not represent 'seeming pure' (IV, 316)—what we take to be a description of idealism—but it is a state where the good is 'dishevell'd', 'as the Vine curls her tendrils' (IV, 306–7). Moreover, the Garden is a place of labour, or as Mrs Lewalsky writes, it is a state of experience:[5]

[4] *Christ and Time: The Primitive Christian Conception of Time and History*, trans. Floyd V. Filson (Philadelphia: Westminster Press, 1964), pp. 81–93.
[5] 'Innocence and Experience in Milton's Eden', *New Essays on Paradise Lost*, ed. Thomas Kranidas (Berkeley: University of California Press, 1969), pp. 86–117.

> *Adam*, well may we labor still to dress
> This Garden, still to tend Plant, Herb and Flow'r,
> Our pleasant task enjoin'd, but till more hands
> Aid us, the work under our labor grows,
> Luxurious by restraint; what we by day
> Lop overgrown, or prune, or prop, or bind,
> One night or two with wanton growth derides
> Tending to wild. Thou therefore now advise
> Or hear what to my mind first thoughts present,
> Let us divide our labors, thou where choice
> Leads thee, or where most needs, whether to wind
> The Woodbine round this Arbor, or direct
> The clasping Ivy where to climb, while I
> In yonder Spring of Roses intermixt
> With Myrtle, find what to redress till Noon:
>
> (IX, 205-19)

Thus, even in the Garden, the condition of things is 'inter-mixt'. For the same reason that Adam's ideal is conversation with his like, his intermixing, the ideal of the Garden is 'tending to wild' in the intermingling of plants, herbs, and flowers. The ideal, then, is to be found in the concrete aspects of nature as it is to be found in the concrete interactions of Adam and Eve. Similarly, history is, potentially, a labour of love, which posits real and concrete events as the material of redemption and salvation: no false prophets, then, no miraculous intervention (not after the Flood, in any case), rather, the meticulous, patient, courageous, and concrete *work* of man ushering in 'New Heaven, New Earth'.

(ii) Ambiguities

Although the pastoral had traditionally been associated with innocence, particularly an escape into innocence, the form was greatly altered by Sidney and Spenser, among others, who displaced the shepherd from his idyllic landscape. Inhabiting the pastoral after this transformation, are ambiguous characters overcome by desire, ruled by the dominant passion of love. The ambiguity is all encompassing in Sidney's *Arcadia*, where desire determines the object of worship, a natural

expectation, and also, the identity of the chivalric lover in that
the lover's strategy requires that he disguise himself as man or
woman in order to be close to the object of veneration. The
ambivalent identity of the characters in the *Arcadia*, based as it
is on the desire for sexual conquest, receives an even more
explicit portrayal by Spenser.

In the first book of the *Faerie Queene*, for instance, the hero's
early sense of purpose, his belief in the purity of his intentions
in the service of Una (which, ironically, serves to separate the
couple after the dream fostered by Archimago), in short, his
calm assurance in his mission and of his identity as warfaring
Christian knight, are revealed as illusions. The Redcrosse
Knight is but another 'changeling boy' caught in the pastoral
woods of error. What characterizes the hero's primary misconception is his belief in his own autonomy, that is, his belief in an
intransitive self unaffected by others. This misconception, in
turn, fosters the hero's desire to be the best knight in 'faerie'
land in establishing his sovereign autonomy over others.
Victory over others serves to liberate the self as autonomous
being. However attractive this goal may seem, the experience
described by Spenser argues, to the contrary, that the achieving
of autonomy goes hand in hand with a progressive revelation
of despair, illustrated by the imprisonment of the Redcrosse
Knight by Orgoglio.

In Spenser's terms, the Redcrosse Knight's security, which
he believes to be an autonomous identity, is nothing else than
pride, and the consequences are nearly disastrous but for the
intervention of King Arthur, symbol of monarchical order and
balance. Imprisoned by his own pride, the hero conceives of
himself as the 'son of Fortune', and bewails the unreliability of
the world and of those surrounding him. Controlled by pride,
he discovers the world as a place of mutability; his blindness is
complete when he transforms his own plight as 'changeling
boy' (the unconscious reality of his belief in autonomy) to an
indictment of the world as changeable place. His strategy is to
resist by any means acknowledging his own responsibility for
his condition, and this is achieved by conceiving of himself as
victim.

Thus, the world lives up to its initial characterization at the
beginning of the poem: a state of plague, of the confounding of

good by evil as the product of a deceptive art which the hero
sets out to redress. All the hero's actions to Canto VIII confirm
this earlier indictment. Consequently, for the hero to serve
Una, the one, true image of his desire for autonomy, is for
him, as well, to substantiate his perception of the world as a
plague-ridden place. Under the sign of the plague, the world is
depicted as a state of undifferentiation and the hero's role is to
transform this condition, one which stands for the identity of
good and evil, into a difference sustained by his autonomy and
superiority. Nevertheless, the mainspring of pastoral is the
belief in equality,[6] and, to the extent that this is so, it is at odds
with the hero's desire. The ambiguity created by this distinction
is admirably illustrated by a passage from *Don Quixote*, when
the knight errant, lulled by the pastoral atmosphere created by
the goatherds (the displacement of shepherds by goatherds is,
of course, an ironic reflection on Cervantes' conception of the
condition of the pastoral in his own time), says to his companion:

> That thou may'st understand, *Sancho*, the Benefits of Knight-
> Errantry, and how the meanest Retainers to it have a fair
> Prospect of being speedily esteem'd and honour'd by the
> World, 'tis my Pleasure that thou sit thee down by me, in the
> Company of these good People; and that there be no Differ-
> ence now observ'd between thee and me, thy natural Lord
> and Master; that thou eat in the same Dish, and drink in the
> same Cup: For it may be said of Knight-Errantry, as of
> Love, that it makes all Things equal.[7]

This is an interlude and a pretence in the relationship which
ordinarily holds between the knight and his squire, for precisely, since the decline of the Golden Age, the reality of
knighthood is *difference*, the difference of 'Lord and Master'
and squire, who set the pattern for Hegel's famous paradigm of
master/slave. But as Don Quixote goes on to say in this section,
it is an ambivalent difference, since its aim is to reintroduce
equality into the world. We will quote the remainder of the

[6] William Empson, *Some Versions of Pastoral* (New York: New Directions,
1968), pp. 3–23. Empson maintains that the pastoral is 'a natural expression
for a sense of injustice', p. 17.

[7] All quotations are from *Don Quixote*, trans. Peter Motteux, rev. Ozell
(New York: Airmont Publishing, 1967), p. 66.

M: SR—E

passage with few deletions, because it is extremely suggestive
for our purposes:

> And now Don *Quixote* having satisfy'd his Appetite, he took a
> Handful of Acorns, and looking earnestly upon 'em; O
> happy Age, cry'd he, which our first Parents call'd the Age of
> Gold! not because Gold, so much ador'd in this Iron-Age,
> was then easily purchas'd, but because those two fatal
> Words, Mine and Thine, were Distinctions unknown to the
> People of those fortunate Times; for their Sustenance,
> needed only to lift their Hands, and take it from the sturdy
> Oak. . . . All then was Union, all Peace, all Love and
> Friendship in the World. . . . Lovers then express'd the
> Passion of their Souls in the unaffected Language of the
> Heart, with the native Plainness and Sincerity. . . . But in
> this degenerate Age, Fraud and a Legion of Ills infecting the
> World, no Virtue can be safe, no Honour be secure; while
> wanton Desires, diffus'd into the Hearts of men, corrupt the
> strictest Watches, and the closest Retreats; which, though as
> intricate and unknown as the Labyrinth of *Crete*, are no
> security for Chastity. Thus that Primitive Innocence being
> vanish'd, and Oppression daily prevailing, there was a
> Necessity to oppose the Torrent of Violence: For which
> Reason the Order of Knighthood-Errant was instituted.[8]

In the Golden Age, the ruling sign is 'similarity': everyone
is the same and everyone wants the same things. There is no
'Mine and Thine', consequently, similarity and equality. Don
Quixote's context, however, his 'degenerate age', is characterized by discord, quests, possessions, violence, and difference.
What Don Quixote does not realize is that he, and more
particularly, his role as knight errant, is a sign of the violence
and discord which he laments; that is to say, that he is an
expression of the violence he inveighs against as characteristic
of the age of iron. At first sight, his contradictory stance is
somewhat ameliorated by his role as lover whose intention is
to destroy difference insofar as difference serves to separate him
from his mistress. But even in this context, his status is less than
clear, since the mistress (we see this in Ariosto and Spenser as

[8] *Don Quixote*, pp. 67–8.

well)[9] is more often than not the very issue which will distinguish one knight from another. Don Quixote maintains that he fights to protect the innocent; as often, however, he fights to keep the honour of Dulcinea untarnished. In short, the mistress, in being desirable, creates a situation of conflict where two knights will fight for her favours. Thus, she becomes the source for the ultimate separation of good from evil, victor from loser, and, in this way, she becomes the motive force of further difference and contention which creates a condition 'as intricate and unknown as the Labyrinth of *Crete*'.

Paradise Lost, similarly, stages these heroic contradictions in the epic machinery of poem. But of primary importance, to begin with, is the fact that the Garden, a symbol of unity and equality, a variant on the Golden Age trope, contains two unequal beings. The fall, it has been argued, is largely the result of Eve's awareness and dissatisfaction with her difference from her Adam.[10] Additionally, Satan's temptation gives Eve the opportunity of becoming Adam's equal, and, of course, it accomplishes this end with unforeseen results. Eve becomes Adam's equal, but in the sense in which the 'plague' makes everyone equally susceptible to infection and death. By contrast, the bliss of Paradise depends on degree and respect for place: any break in the hierarchy means its total contamination. With this in mind, we can appreciate the extent to which *Paradise Lost* is concerned with the analysis of equality and inequality, of identity and difference. In this respect, the 'other' worlds of Heaven and Hell and this world come together.

We rarely fail to emphasize that the Satanic character is formed on the pattern of Homeric heroes like Prometheus, Achilles, and so forth. But, as often, we fail to see that Satan, as heroic character, is formed by a prior stance, that of unrequited lover,[11] a characterization which comes through with particular force at the end of Book IV in Gabriel's statement to Satan: 'who more than thou / Once fawn'd, and cring'd, and servilely ador'd / Heav'n's awful Monarch?' (958-60). At the

[9] *Cf.* Eugenio Donato, ' "Per Selve e Boscherecci Labirinti": Desire and Narrative Structure in Ariosto's *Orlando Furioso*,' *Barroco*, 4 (1972).

[10] Rozenberg, 'Amour, Don, Sujétion', pp. 130-32.

[11] See John Steadman, *Milton and the Renaissance Hero* (Oxford: Clarendon Press, 1967), pp. 108-36, for a discussion of 'amor'.

root of Satan's heroism is his role as lover and his desire to be chosen by God, not an unnatural wish, since his desire is an imitation of heavenly love. He is surprised to find his love unworthy (it is the model for Cain's later discomfiture when his sacrifice is found unacceptable; his rejection, like Satan's, is transformed into violence). Rejected, he becomes a rebel. This stance is not intended as a final position, but should be understood in terms of the characteristic sulking of the lover. This response is intended to signal to God Satan's displeasure in the hope that his show of feeling will lead to a reconciliation.

The rebellion, then, simply indicates the extent of Satan's love and attachment to God and the continuation of his desire to be noticed.[12] Satan desires recognition, a recognition which he enjoyed in the love of the Father prior to the appearance of the Son and which he will attempt to gain at any cost, even at the price of Hell, once his position is usurped.

Not able to achieve recognition as an equal, he will, nevertheless, find a way to remain in God's eye as an unequal in a relationship of alterity.[13] It is only in this way that Satan's frenzied activity in Hell and his laborious journey to the earth—an undertaking which he knows will not defeat God but simply pester him—makes any sense. He will work to remain forever in God's eye; he attempted this in his rejection of the Son in Heaven, and on earth he will find a way to disrupt the possibility of another of God's loves:

> There went a fame in Heav'n that he ere long
> Intended to create, and therein plant
> A generation, whom his choice regard
> Should favor *equal* to the Sons of Heaven:
>
> (I, 651–54, my italics)

It has been noticed before that when Satan arrives on earth, he sets up the first love triangle.[14] He comes in disguise, but

[12] See René Girard, 'The Stranger Retried', *PMLA*, 79 (1964), pp. 530–531, for a parallel reading with particular stress on the reactive nature of juvenile delinquency.

[13] The situation is similar to that of Dostoyevski's *Notes From the Underground*. Tzvetan Todorov has dealt with this subject in a paper delivered at McGill University in 1971: 'Le Recit Souterrain de Dostoievski'.

[14] Cope, p. 56. In actuality, the first love triangle is in Heaven; the second is in Hell. The earthly triangle, for this reason, is merely a redun-

at heart Satan is always the lover. The disguises show the extent to which he will go to find favour with Eve, and, through her, to be recognized by God. It is a desperate condition, and we can understand the sympathy which has been shown Satan, often for the wrong reasons, but reasons which always take us back to his original rejection as lover. On this basis, we can explore the nature of Satan's disguises, and, particularly, we can come to understand Milton's delineation of Satan as a hero. For, if nothing else, Satan is heroic. He represents a heroism, however, which is based on his peculiar blindness as lover.

Acting every inch the hero, after he has been nominated by the council of Hell to undertake the arduous journey to earth, Satan encounters Sin and Death at the gates of Hell. He does not *recognize* his paramour, and only escapes sudden death because she remembers him. The lesson is plain: heroism is only possible when the hero is allowed to forget the real cause which motivates him, and, moreover, heroism is, singularly, a device which fosters misconceptions.[15] Satan has been hurt in his love, and there are two alternatives forced upon him by this rejection: either, the inaction we find him in at the beginning of the poem, or, heroic behaviour. To dwell on the memory of his humiliation is to be fated to inaction and the violent cries of the damned—one can recall the characteristic stance of the Petrarchan lover forever lamenting his unrequited love. Able to block the painful memory, on the other hand, the hero can act and act all the more courageously, because he has nothing to lose, seeing that his behaviour is originally dictated by his extreme consciousness that everything is lost. Satan is blinded by the apparition of the Son, but he blinds himself far more through a heroism which he uses as a shield to fend off the truth of his condition. Sin opens the gates of Hell for Satan because she remembers and, because as sin, she has nothing to hide.

---

dancy, although it is potentially recuperative if Christ is substituted for Satan.

[15] E. M. W. Tillyard, *Milton* (New York: Barnes and Noble, 1967), p. 229. Tillyard observes that Satan is a sensualist. Belial, in *Paradise Regained*, offers confirmation to this charge in his suggestion that Christ be tempted by a woman. What is relevant here is not so much the characterization of Belial as Satan's emphatic rejection of his sexual temptation.

(iii) Rivalries

Returning to our previous discussion of the pastoral context
of heroism, Satan, as hero, desires to be different, and, by
virtue of this difference, secure the love of God. The logic of
his position, however, forces him to create the first lover's Hell,
a surreptitious state of non-difference where all are apparently
equal, but in an equality fostered by the plague—a word
which has suggestive sexual connotations in the Renaissance.
His task, throughout the poem, will be a linguistic and sexual
contamination, in bringing the plague to the earth and from
the earth to Heaven, thus introducing a degenerate identity in
the perversion of love.

Although Satan attempts to maintain his difference, it is
not an easy matter as seen in the involuntary utterances of his
soliloquies. He is also affected by the plague, seeing that he is
all plague and represents a state of non-differentiation, the
diffusion of the non-difference of good and evil, which is the
metaphoric sense of the plague.

Nevertheless, Satan is a hero, if the hero is recognized as
one who would have others pay for his faults, and, in doing so,
erase the memory of an earlier humiliation and rejection. In
opposition to Satan's stance is Christ in the role of true Son,
who does not need the defences of heroism, since he is accepted,
loved, and doing the Father's work. The heroism of Satan, on
the other hand, is nothing else than setting himself against
the Father as rival. Thus, what begins as an adoration of the
Father, an adoration which, interestingly, is fostered by the
Father's command to do as he does in imitating his love,
becomes the source of rivalry, once the imitation is directed to
an object. Imitating the Father's desire, that is to say, to want
what he wants, is for Satan to situate himself as the Father's
rival.

As René Girard says in his analysis of Oedipus, a character
who has monumental problems with the father:

The son does what the father does, he desires what the father
desires without realizing the threat which he poses in the
father's universe. . . . Nothing, then, prepares the son for the
violence of the father. The son cannot understand that his

fate depends not on the law but on the father's desire. . . .
The interdiction which strikes the son is incomprehensible;
this is why he creates between the father and himself an
infinite distance. The son is literally deported by the violence
of the father. This original difference, of *dis-fere*, of aliena-
tion, of dispersion, of dissemination, of differentiation is the
matrix of all 'values.' Constrained by the parental obstacle
to choose between the father and himself, the son can only
choose the father. He excludes himself from the kingdom.
He judges himself unworthy of succeeding the father and
disinherits himself. He constitutes himself as the original
scapegoat.[16]

Satan remains unconscious to all of this, because he transforms
the Father into a supreme obstacle, in terms of the 'ancient
Tyranny of Heaven', the source of an incomprehensible law
which determines that damnation is the Son's destiny to the
extent that he rivals and wars against the Father. Warfare and
heroic behaviour are, consequently, expressions of the blindness
generated by the conception of the Father as obstacle.

At the beginning of *Paradise Lost*, Satan is at an 'infinite
distance' from the Father, and he attempts to traverse this
distance with great difficulty, since the journey is fraught with
obstacles of his own making. Satan, in short, faced with his
own obstacles, becomes himself an obstacle, the supreme
obstacle to faith, because he reads the law as interdiction and
fails to acknowledge the promise of the Father's acceptance; the
complementary meaning of the law handed down in the
Mosaic covenant. The law is both an obstacle (interdiction) and
a sign of God's choice of Israel as his 'promised Seed', and it

---

[16] Girard, 'Symétrie et Dissymétrie dans le Mythe d'Oedipe', p. 106:
'Le fils fait ce que fait le père, il désire ce que le père désire sans soupçonner
la menace qu'il fait peser sur l'univers du père. . . . Rien, donc, ne prépare
le fils à la violence du père. Le fils ne peut pas soupçonner que ce que lui
destine non pas la loi mais le désir du père. . . . L'interdit qui frappe le fils est
incompréhensible; c'est pourquoi il creuse entre le père et lui une distance
infinie. Le fils est littéralement dé-porté par la violence du père. Cette
différence originelle, de *dis fere*, éloigner, disperser, disséminer, différer, est
la matrice de toute "valeur." Contraint par l'obstacle paternel à choisir
entre le père et lui-même, le fils ne peut que choisir le père. Il s'exclut lui-
même du royaume. Il se juge inapte à succéder au père, à jamais déshérité.
Il se constitue en émissaire originel.'

is the manner in which it is read that determines individual destiny

It is important to see that the earlier analysis of the sign as beginning and end of interpretation joins, at this point, with Girard's reading of the law. As he writes:

> In the western world, there is no law. There is but the incomprehensible shock of contradictory imperatives. The division of the lawful and the unlawful is always performed on an empirical base. The superego is always an illegitimate and precarious substitution that the son erects to escape from the *skandalon* (scandal). This text of Freud's (on the Oedipus complex) rejoins the great works of Kafka on the silence of the law, source of the son's misfortunes and unhappiness.[17]

When Adam in Book X attempts to understand his 'sentence', he is faced with the contradictory injunction of 'deathless Death' (798) and concludes:

> that were to make
> Strange contradiction, which God to himself
> Impossible is held, as Argument
> Of weakness, not of power.
>
> (798–801)

This is precisely the point, however, in that eternal damnation does make the Father contradictory, 'as Argument / Of weakness, not of power'.

But Adam's confusion is due to his ignorance (he is told at the beginning of Book X by the Son, but, apparently, is either inattentive or too busy seeking a scapegoat to notice), that the Father has already devised a plan (as early as Book III) to harmonize his law through the Son as knowledgeable and willing sacrifice, a plan which will put an end to the law as obstacle once and for all.

[17] Ibid., p. 133: 'Dans le monde occidental, il n'y a pas de loi. Il n'y a que le heurt incompréhensible d'impératifs contradictoires. Le partage du licite et de l'illicite se fait toujours sur des bases empiriques. Le Surmoi est un substitut toujours bâtard et précaire que le fils essaie d'échaffauder pour échapper au *skandalon*. Ce texte de Freud rejoint les grands textes de Kafka sur le silence de la loi, cause des malheurs du fils.'

The Son's knowledge contrasts with Satan's blindness, as his acceptance of his role as willing sacrifice is opposed to Satan's repetitive search for a scapegoat who can effect his catharsis. So long as Satan wishes to maintain himself in a position of radical difference, he fails to see the truth of the Son's position as identity in the image of the Father. We can understand his refusal, because to be a true son is far more difficult than to be a renegade and apostate: it requires an adoration which is all-encompassing in the willing sacrifice and the passion of the cross. This, in Milton's eyes, is indeed an exceptional heroism, because it is an act which is fully conscious of the price to be paid.

(iv) Reciprocity: mirrors

Milton's handling of the specific heroic material in the 'War in Heaven' in Book VI is balanced in the mirrored structure, by the knowledge and discrimination of the creation in Book VII. To repeat, Satan's heroism depends on his misconstruction and misunderstanding of his peculiar motivation. Consequently, the heroic stance cannot be redressed by achieving and accumulating greater deeds because these actions merely serve to deepen the deception, but only by understanding the source of heroic courage. Thus, Milton's prescription for undermining false heroism is knowledge: the particular knowledge of the source and motivation of the heroic. Such it is to be 'lowly wise'. To attempt, on the other hand, to defeat the hero on his own ground is to suffer reciprocally his blindness and rage which alienates one from God.

Thus, the 'War in Heaven' is a situation where, upon entering the conflict, the good angels are transformed into creatures no better and no worse than those they stand against, and this is why they are unable to dispose of the rebel forces. The reader, of course, persists in seeing difference where identity exists, in seeing strength where all are weak, in perceiving good where evil prevails, and, because of this, he fails to see the point of the narrative, or, at best, finds it extremely muddled.[18] This is because, as readers, we are living the myth which the narrative

[18] See Fish, *Surprised by Sin*, pp. 180–83; he gives numerous examples of the confusion of the critics on the 'War in Heaven'.

renders suspicious, that is to say, that we persist in thinking of
virtue or evil as fixed essences which depend on an a priori
judgement. To be in God's camp is to be good and partake of
his infinite strength, while to be a rebel is to be weak with no
strength but one's own.

In addition, we experience the episode from the end, and,
since the end seriously contaminates the beginning (the story
is told after the fact by a partisan angel), we are compelled to
read differences in the slanted nomenclature of Raphael who
calls one angel good (they are on the same side) and another
evil. Is it surprising, then, that Raphael and the victorious
angels, not to mention numerous critics, misunderstand the meaning of Christ's miraculous apparition at the end of the battle?

One can admit that to a degree the plan of the 'War in
Heaven' is intended to foster a certain amount of reverence
and awe over the Son's power and righteousness, but Raphael's
reading of the event is suspicious when it transforms the Son
into another epic hero. The Son may seem a hero, he may
appear as an exceptional warrior, but to believe this is to forget
that the Son never actually touches any of the rebel forces;
rather, he blinds them and it is this blindness which drives
them back. The Son also sends down thunder, but this is reversed thunder, because the Son is a mirror reflecting the violence created in the conflict of the 'War in Heaven'. What
defeats the rebels, then, is only partially understood if it is
seen as the individual heroic prowess of the Son; far more
important in the victory in Heaven is the Son's nature as
mirror and the fact that the Satanic troops are defeated at the
moment they take up arms against the Father. The passage in
which this defeat takes place deserves a closer view:

> Full soon
> Among them he arriv'd; in his right hand
> Grasping ten thousand Thunders, which he sent
> Before him, such as thir Souls infix'd
> Plagues; they astonisht all resistance lost,
> All courage; down thir idle weapons dropp'd;
> O'er Shields and Helms, and helmed heads he rode
> Of Thrones and mighty Seraphim prostrate,
> That wish't the Mountains now might be again

Thrown on them as a shelter from his ire.
Nor less on either side tempestuous fell
His arrows, from the fourfold-visag'd Four,
Distinct with eyes, and from the living Wheels,
Distinct alike with multitude of eyes;
One Spirit in them rul'd, and every eye
Glar'd lightning, and shot forth pernicious fire
Among th' accurst, that wither'd all thir strength,
And of thir wonted vigor left them drain'd,
Exhausted, spiritless, afflicted, fall'n.
Yet half his strength he put not forth, . . .

(VI, 834–53)

The Son is only angry because his nature is perfectly reflective. He does not infix plagues which were not originally present in the rebels' first act of apostasy; he does not blind them and drive them back, because their wounds are self-inflicted, following the model of Satan who first 'could not bear / Through pride that sight, and thought himself impair'd'. The Son's eyes, a 'multitude of eyes', express his ire; they condemn with sight the fallen angels. In this sense, he is doubly reflective, as mirror and as fully conscious and knowledgeable of the ways of sin and heroism. In a word, he shows the rebels the concrete cause of their rebellion which the warfare had momentarily allowed them to forget. And it is through the cause in being made to see the folly and uselessness of their undertaking, that they are ultimately vanquished.[19]

More generally, the 'War in Heaven' represents a movement from difference to identity. Apparently, unlike each other, the two forces, as they enter into battle, become progressively indistinguishable—so much so, that neither side can win, without the external agency of the Son who acts through a distance which represents his power. For the violence of the war, like all violence, transforms the inequality of good and evil into a mixture of angels who are all equally confounded by their own proper violence until they create a state similar to that of Chaos. Violence does not distinguish, even though the parties believe it does while bearing allegiance to a heroic code;

---

[19] This psychological interpretation is supported by Milton's *Art of Logic* in *Works*, *XI*, p. 59.

rather, it changes everyone directly involved in the violence
into antagonistic alter-egos. (This doubling characteristic will
be discussed in greater detail in the next chapter.)

Violence is self-blinding. One may feel, in a frenzy of
violence, that it is the other side which is being punished, but
the nature of violence is reciprocity. The damage is equal on
both sides, as both parties submit to the round of suspicions,
accusations, and counter-accusations (the taunting of the
angels in the 'War of Heaven' which follows the accusations of
Abdiel and Satan), heroic postures, the coarseness of recriminations, not to mention a general and progressive coarsening of
character. (This transformation, of course, will serve Satan well
when he becomes the pre-eminent politician in Hell.) How
else can the Son's meekness be seen in this deteriorating light
than as 'ire' where 'every eye / Glar'd lightning' (my emphasis)?

The 'War in Heaven' is discord and sets the pattern of all
future contentions as the 'first / Daughter of Sin' (X, 707–8).
Adam and Eve, for instance, after the fall, 'in mutual accusation spent / The fruitless hours, but neither self-condemning, /
And of thir vain contest appear'd no end' (IX, 1187–9). Like
the 'War in Heaven', the discord of Adam and Eve will be
resolved by the Son in a merciful judgement.

The Son's judgement is no obstacle meant to lead to further
recriminations and accusations (we recall how quickly he
silences Adam's accusation of Eve in Book X); rather, it spells
the end of judgement and the heroic pretensions which are
founded on the belief in personal righteousness. Moreover,
the Son's judgement is not an obstacle, because it is *revelation*
in the puritan sense of the word. It is a revelation of the truth
of judgement which is self-incrimination. In the realization of
this, Adam and Eve can live at peace with each other; any
other way, as Adam shows in his own self-recrimination in
Book X, is to be in 'wandering mazes lost'. From the providential point of view, Christ shows that the *end* of judgement is
mercy.

(v) The solitary way

To summarize, the truth of violence, contrary to the hero's
belief, is the plague, a state of non-difference where all are

equally guilty of the excesses of violence. This is ignored, as Girard says, because violence is experienced from the point of view of a myth of expulsion whose function is to introduce a difference, the *difference*, where none exists and whose secondary characteristic is to create its own proper misconception.[20] The expulsion must be made to seem inevitable, whereas, caught up in violence, anyone will do as a sacrificial offering. Finally, the choice of scapegoat is an arbitrary one: the expulsion is seen differently, however, because of the contamination of the structure by the myth in the sense in which the myth is an interpretation of difference. What this means in terms of the practical problem of *Paradise Lost* is that we read a story (a myth) told by Raphael who has already undergone the experience being recounted and, because of this, we are submitted to his interpretation of the events. He contaminates the story by reading the expulsion of Satan into his characterization, thus transforming his identity to the 'good' angels into a paramount difference: he is the proud one; he is the apostate; in short, he is *evil*.

Similarly, in *Oedipus Rex*, the characterization of Oedipus, contaminated by a mythic interpretation, emphasizes his nature as regicide, patricide, and, finally, as incestuous: acts with a similar grounding in the destruction of the difference between parent and child. For the same reason, Satan is incestuous, or at least, is responsible for the incestuous relationship of Sin and Death, as he is, in addition, a potential regicide and patricide. But, unlike Oedipus, the characterization of Satan is never an exact one. From Satan's point of view, not Raphael's, it is more fantasy than fact. Satan would be a Greek hero, if he could, but must settle for his fantasies of difference. For the Christian, evil is not real, or, if real, it is certainly not exceptional (different), but all too common.

To see evil in this way is to destroy its epic pretensions and to show that the antidote to false heroism is knowledge, the precise knowledge that it is the deceptive nature of the expulsion of the scapegoat which is responsible for the illusion of difference. Thus, to understand *Paradise Lost*, it must be approached with an acute sensitivity to the stumbling-block of difference. Reason, right reason, is nothing else than the

[20] Girard, 'Symétrie et Dissymétrie dans le Mythe d'Oedipe,' p. 101.

distinction of true from false difference, and the import of the
books which follow the 'War in Heaven' is a schooling in
difference.

In eliminating the difference between man and woman, Eve
sets off a chain reaction, causing Adam to destroy the difference
between man and God, an action which has the interesting
effect of transforming Adam and Eve into the likeness of beasts
at the end of Book IX. In a way, of course, God is partly
responsible for the problems which arise from difference to
the extent that the divine system, whether in Heaven or on
Earth in the pre-fallen state, is one of difference, hierarchy, and
degree sustained by a divine interdiction.

In terms of divine providence, however, this law is intended
as a partial solution to a puzzling problem. Finally, it is meant
to be surpassed by the interpretation of the Son. For difference,
he substitutes the identity of a God made man. Not a God made
by man, not man fantasizing his God-like image and transforming himself in his ignorance into a hero who rivals God,
but the God who made man 'lowly wise'. God, himself, abolishes
the difference between Godhead and man in sending his own
Son to be man. This is sufficient cause for happiness, and, we
might add, for 'justification'.

At this juncture, however, it is necessary to be especially
careful; it is necessary to know what it means when something,
an idea, an event, an interpretation, makes us feel good. As
Nietzsche writes in *Beyond Good and Evil*, 'Take care, philosophers and friends of knowledge, and beware of martyrdom.'[21]
In *Paradise Lost*, what makes us feel good is all too often the
easy way, the superficial interpretation, the unconscious substitutions of good and evil. The way is not an easy one: freedom
and independence come to very few according to Books XI and
XII. Again, Nietzsche supplies an interesting gloss:

> Independence is for the very few; it is a privilege of the
> strong. And whoever attempts it even with the best right
> but without inner constraint proves that he is probably not
> only strong, but also daring to the point of recklessness. He
> enters into a labyrinth, he multiplies a thousandfold the
> dangers which life brings with it in any case, not the least

[21] *Beyond Good and Evil*, Part II, 25, p. 225.

of which is that no one can see how and where he loses his way, becomes lonely, and is torn piecemeal by some minotaur of conscience. Supposing one like that comes to grief, this happens so far from the comprehension of men that they neither feel it nor sympathize. And he cannot go back any longer. Nor can he go back to the pity of men.[22]

We have learned in *Paradise Lost* what it means to wander without a guide in the mazy labyrinth of the poem, but have we learned—a far more difficult lesson—that the truth is always the truth at one's expense, that it is always the truth against oneself? Certainly, this is the intent of the Son's statement in Book X: 'but thou Know'st / Whoever judg'd, the worst on mee must light' (72–3). Because of this, the truth is difficult to bear; it requires courage to be independent and to sustain this truth against oneself, since no one will know and no one will sympathize if one *falls* under the burden.

Quoting Voltaire, Nietzsche writes concerning man's search for the truth, 'il ne cherche le vrai que pour faire le bien'[23]— a beautifully ambiguous phrase, and earlier, he says in a passage which sounds very much like the Milton of the invocations:

Our highest insights must—and should—sound like follies and sometimes like crimes when they are heard without permission by those who are not predisposed and predestined for them, The difference between the exoteric and the esoteric, formerly known to philosophers—among the Indians as among the Greeks, Persians and Muslims, in short, wherever one believed in an order of rank and *not* in equality and equal rights—does not so much consist in this, that the exoteric approach comes from outside and sees, estimates, measures, and judges from the outside, not the inside: what is much more essential is that the exoteric approach sees things from below, the esoteric looks *down from above*. . . .

What serves the higher type of men as nourishment or delectation must almost be poison for a very different and inferior type. The virtues of the common man might perhaps signify vices and weaknesses in a philosopher. . . . There are

22 Part II, 29, pp. 229–30.
23 Part II, 35, p. 237.

books that have opposite values for soul and health, depending on whether the lower soul, the lower vitality, or the
higher and more vigorous ones turn to them: in the former
case, these books are dangerous and lead to crumbling and
disintegration; in the latter, herald's cries that call the
bravest to *their* courage. Books for all the world are always
foul smelling books: the smell of small people cling to them.
Where the people eat and drink, even where they venerate, it
usually stinks. One should not go to church if one wants to
breathe *pure* air.[24]

The passage is extremely suggestive for understanding Milton's
intention in *Paradise Lost*, his strategy of ascent and descent,
his call for a privileged audience—'fit audience, though few'—
and his desire to:

> drive far off the barbarous dissonance
> Of *Bacchus* and his Revellers, the Race
> Of that wild Rout that tore the *Thracian* Bard
> In *Rhodope*, where Woods and Rocks had Ears
> To rapture, till the savage clamor drown'd
> Both Harp and Voice;
>
> (VII, 32–7)

As well, it recalls Milton's judgement of the clergy and of state
religion in the tracts on reformation. In short, *Paradise Lost* is
intended as a 'herald's cries that call the bravest to *their*
courage'.

In this 'egalitarian' age, there are difficulties in accepting
Milton's vision as the basis of true difference. Perhaps, it
softens the blow somewhat to realize that in Miltonic terms
difference is not a privilege of caste, but follows from the
courageous pursuit of truth. The pursuit, as much as the truth
itself, is the end of wisdom, or, expressed differently, truth is
located in the process of attaining knowledge. In this sense, the
degree of suffering of God's prophets is a sign of their calling as
their life is witness to their endless quest for truth which ultimately reveals the sign of difference in an 'extra-moral' sense.

[24] Part II, 30, pp. 232–3.

PART III
'They also serve'

8

Samson as 'medicine man': the play of surfaces

> Terrible experiences pose the riddle whether the person who has them is not terrible.
>
> Nietzsche, *Beyond Good and Evil*

(i) Roles

Samson is a hero of legendary proportions, famous for his strength, for his skill in war against the Philistines, and, for this reason, Milton characterizes him in terms of the contradictions consistent with a violent temperament. This he does, in part, by patterning Samson on the Satanic model with the emphasis on the obstacle created by the father, Manoa, his disappointing marriages, and his heroic conduct: three apparently dissimilar and contradictory relationships.

The initial impression of Samson is of discontinuity: his roles as faithful son, loving husband, and heroic leader of his tribe against the Philistines are contradictory, since to be a loyal son means to please Manoa in fighting the Philistines and also it means to resist marrying women outside his tribe and, in particular, it means not marrying the Philistine woman, Dalila. Conversely, if Samson is to be a loving husband, he must go against his father's wishes and cease his warring against his wife's tribe. In general, then, it is these contradictions which are encountered at the beginning of the play. Samson's heroic behaviour is at odds with the possibility of human relationships and it is denoted by a special sign: 'voices from above'. In addition, it is these 'voices'—an expression of the discord between the tribes of Israel into which Samson is injected—which create dissension between his father and his wife, since they counsel his marriage to 'strange' women and his defeat of Israel's oppressors, the same group into which he marries.

These voices (Samson's inspiration) must be questioned, for they are the basis of his heroism and the contradiction of his roles. Are the voices responsible for Samson's doubleness?

> *Chorus:* Tax not divine disposal; wisest Men
> Have err'd, and by bad Women been deceiv'd;
> And shall again, pretend they ne'er so wise.
> Deject not then so overmuch thyself,
> Who hast of sorrow thy full load besides;
> Yet truth to say, I oft have heard men wonder
> Why thou shouldst wed *Philistian* women rather
> Than of thy own tribe fairer, or as fair,
> At least of thy own Nation, and as noble.
>   *Samson:* The first I saw at *Timna*, and she pleas'd
> Mee, not my Parents, that I sought to wed,
> The daughter of an Infidel: they knew not
> That what I motion'd was of God; I knew
> From intimate impulse, and therefore urg'd
> The Marriage on; that by occasion hence
> I might begin *Israel's* Deliverance,
> The work to which I was divinely call'd;
> She proving false, the next I took to Wife
> (O that I never had! fond wish too late)
> Was in the Vale of *Sorec*, *Dalila*,
> That specious Monster, my accomplisht snare.
> I thought it lawful from my former act,
> And the same end; still watching to oppress
> *Israel's* oppressors: of what now I suffer
> She was not the prime cause, but I myself,
> Who vanquisht with a peal of words (O weakness!)
> Gave up my fort of silence to a Woman.
>   *Chorus:* In seeking just occasion to provoke
> The *Philistine*, thy Country's Enemy,
> Thou never wast remiss, I bear thee witness:
> Yet *Israel* still serves with all his Sons.
>   (210–40)

Samson's 'intimate impulse' concerns his first marriage; his second marriage is the product of his interpretation of this inspiration: 'I thought it lawful from my former act, / And the same end'. Where Samson goes wrong is in his interpretation, for he reads his marriage to Dalila, one which is not sanctioned by 'intimate impulse', as an opportunity for revenge: 'still watching to oppress / *Israel's* oppressors'. Samson's interpretation is intended to justify an act which has no justification. It does so by channelling his sexual passion for Dalila (his 'accomplisht snare') into a rationale for continuing the tribal antagonism between the House of Dan and the Philistines. This rationalization, as seen in the Chorus's rejoinder, is fully credible to his friends and family. Should we, however, concur in their judgement? Should we participate in Samson's and the Chorus's blindness by ignoring the personal motives which led Samson into his marriages in the first place and which set him against the law of his own tribe? Should we not, on the other hand, emphasize the pettiness of Samson's motivation, all the more so for his wilful disregard of the true nature of his inspiration?

If we look to the majority of critics who have considered Milton's play, we find an audience all too eager to discount the *hero's* short-comings and his all too human character. And, in this judgement, they have recourse to the same scapegoats who serve Samson so well, the Philistines. Thanks to the Philistines, one has no need to think about this play. For, after all, aren't the Philistines the guilty ones; are they not idol-worshippers and perverters of the true faith; are they not evil? If so, is Samson not, by contrast, representative of all goodness victimized by the Satanic forces in the world? Even admitting that Samson is not totally attractive, is he not, it is argued, a *type* of the ultimate righteousness of Christ and, furthermore, is not the miracle which he performs at the temple at Gaza the crucial sign of his acceptance among the 'company of saints and warfaring Christians'? Is he not, in a word, 'good medicine'?

It would be necessary to exclude Dr Johnson and, more recently, William Empson[1] from the list, but, indeed, Milton's Samson has been 'good medicine' for the critics. Milton can be excused for his failure with Dr Johnson; we know from Boswell that Dr Johnson was, at the best of times, a difficult patient.

[1] See *The Lives of the English Poets*, ed. Thorpe, p. 85; William Empson, 'A Defense of Delilah', *SR*, LXVIII (1960), pp. 240–55.

Without speculating on the possible reasons for his intransigence in the face of the curative value of *Samson Agonistes*, we can at least say that Johnson's commentary on *Samson Agonistes* has created a critical tradition which has exalted the play as good Christian morality and teaching. This reaction to Johnson's criticism requires reconsideration, for, unfortunately, the effect of traditional criticism has been to close the text on the note of 'consolation' and instruction. G. A. Welkes has argued that the approach of those conciliatory critics who would re-Christianize Milton's play has been explicitly of a psychological order, and the force of his argument is that the play remains eminently unconvincing on this level,[2] as Dr Johnson himself had realized. So that Milton's 'good medicine' could be bad therapy: more a distortion of symptoms and cures than 'good medicine'. Consequently, our implication in the text and in its message—in short, the stake we have in the play's outcome—needs to be kept in mind as we form judgements on Milton's intent and that of the play's major characters.

If the narrator in *Paradise Lost* can be said to mirror and condition our response to the action of the epic, this being Milton's own version of 'accommodation' to the reader's fallenness, then, it can be argued that the Chorus in *Samson Agonistes* performs a similar function. The equivocation of both the narrator and the Chorus in their response to a shifting scene is indicative of the limitations which Milton imposes on a subjective interpretation of the action. Ultimately, these limitations are those which result from an ideological commitment to a programme, whether that of Puritan morality or the Judaic code, and they are felt in initial readings of either *Paradise Lost* or *Samson* as a problem of tone. In terms of tonality, both the narrator and the Chorus seem to have been contaminated by that most prevalent form of Puritan *hubris*, smugness, and self-righteousness. In short, the Chorus, like the narrator, presents a problem, and to the degree that we identify with either of them, we may be said to have adopted their smugness, and, in turn, to have given up our critical perspective and the responsibility of choice which Milton defines as 'right reason'.

We must admit, nevertheless, that the Chorus conditions our response to the play, for the Chorus undergoes an experience

2 'The Interpretation of *Samson Agonistes*', *HLQ*, 26 (1962–3), pp. 366–7.

similar to our own.[3] Both the Chorus and the audience are
being educated to God's ways by the action of the play, and it
seems probable that the Chorus's catharsis at the end of the
play is intended to record the common response to Samson's
career:

> All is best, though we oft doubt
> What th' unsearchable dispose
> Of Highest Wisdom brings about,
> And ever best found in the close. . . .
>
> With peace and consolation hath dismissed,
> And calm of mind, all passion spent.
>
> (1745–59)

The Chorus and all it represents has been vindicated by
Samson's last heroic action, but one is impelled to recall, at this
point, its earlier anxiety concerning 'Highest Wisdom':

> God of our fathers! what is man,
> That thou towards him with hand so various—
> Or might I say contrarious?—
> Temper'st thy providence through his short course:
> Not evenly, as thou rul'st
> The angelic orders, and the inferior creatures mute
> Irrational and brute?
>
> . . . In fine,
> Just or unjust alike seem miserable,
> For oft alike both come to evil end.
>
> (667–704)

Obviously, the Chorus is as changeable as the conditions it
records. Are we to conclude, then, that it has learned from its
experience and that its consolation is meant to be ours as well?
To put it differently, the question is one of determining the
extent of Milton's didacticism in the play. Is the play, finally,
theology or drama?

[3] See A. S. P. Woodhouse, 'Tragic Effect in *Samson Agonistes*', *Milton:
Modern Essays in Criticism*, p. 451. While agreeing with Professor Woodhouse's characterization of the Chorus, it is necessary to insist on another
aspect of its role as spectators in a theatrical context.

A closer analysis of the Chorus's function is instructive in this respect. The Chorus's role in *Samson* is a double one: to reflect the public morality of spectators at a play and to participate in the action as friends of the hero. In turn, the Chorus gives us, through its double vision, a Samson who is both a private person and a public spectacle. For, however much the Chorus's sympathy for the hero determines its sense of Samson undergoing the rigours of his faith, he remains, for all that, a play, something to be looked at which carries the name of *Samson Agonistes*. In the initial encounter between Samson and the Chorus, the action is deliberately staged through the use of commonplace analogies from Elizabethan drama:

> But who are these? for with joint pace I hear
> The tread of many feet steering this way;
> Perhaps my enemies, who come to stare
> At my affliction, and perhaps to insult—
> Their daily practice to afflict me more.
>
> (110–14)

This passage emphasizes Samson's general evaluation of himself as a fool with respect to others who come to see him and torment him (75–8). But, as well, it distinguishes the theatrical natures of Samson and the Chorus according to their roles as actor and spectator with, additionally, an interesting mistake on Samson's part in his confusion of the Chorus for the enemy, a confusion which will be borne out as the action develops. The Chorus, on the other hand, stages the afflicted Samson in its own moral and theatrical commonplace in seeing him as a 'mirror of our fickle state' (164). Initially, the Chorus stands at a distance: 'let us not break in upon him' (116). Not yet in the same theatrical space as Samson and seeing Samson as a stage representation, the Chorus's judgements are easy. Their next speech, however, brings them into action; 'let us draw nigh' (178); involved in the action as 'friends and neighbors not unknown' (180), the Chorus will have its faith and certainty shaken as it takes on the condition of blindness which underlies the internal action.

What often happens, then, in a reading of the Chorus's catharsis in its last speech is a confusion of the double aspect of its role. While participating in the action, the Chorus can do little more than record their limited perspective as actors. At the end of the play, however, they are again excluded from the action when the theatrical scene shifts to the Philistines' 'spacious theatre' (1605), and, through this device, returned to their original state as spectators. Given this fact, it becomes, indeed, difficult to distinguish the Chorus's moral consolation from the aesthetic dimensions of the play they have attended. In other words, the Chorus's final response stems from the formal characteristics of the drama they observe, in that the play, like any art work, must have a 'close'. Because of this formal necessity for an ending, the play's conflict wil be resolved, and this resolution will produce a sense of 'peace and consolation'. In our desire to be dismissed from the conflict, we should recognize that our identification with the Chorus in its catharsis, one which is encouraged by the identity imposed upon us by the similarity of our roles as spectators, masks a profound uneasiness.

(ii) Alter egos

Every major character in the play is certain of at least one thing: he, and no one else, possesses the truth. Thus, to maintain in the face of the play's accusations and counter-accusations that a particular character (Dalila, for instance) is 'by definition false'[4] is to conceive of Milton's play as theology and not theatre. One should take Milton at his word in the Preface to the play, when he says that he is, in fact, following the best models so as to write an effective tragedy. The debasement and questioning of character in *Samson Agonistes* may not be as extreme as that found in Webster's plays or in Shakespeare's *Troilus and Cressida*, but it is, nevertheless, a fact that at the low ebb which the play presents it is difficult to find either of the opposing parties particularly attractive. Consequently, to interpret *Samson Agonistes* as an allegorical warfare between the 'children of light' and the 'children of darkness', or, in terms of the play itself, a battle between good Israelites and corrupt Philistines, is to live the myth which the play, if it is at all successful, demystifies. It is, to put it differently, to see the

4 Welkes, 'The Interpretation of *Samson Agonistes*', p. 371.

superiorities, hierarchies, and oppositions guaranteed by the myth—in short, to see differences—where similarity and reciprocity reign.

The conflict of *Samson Agonistes* and the crisis which the play represents is the result of an essential loss of difference. This the Chorus knows, although it is unable to give it sufficient emphasis while speaking from the vantage point of its own myth: 'Just or unjust alike seem miserable / For oft alike both come to evil end.' In terms of the fundamental similarity generated by the conflict of the play, it is possible to see *Samson Agonistes* as the endless oscillation between two warring factions. One of the parties will be victorious, we are assured, because the play will end on one of the oscillations.

Structurally, *Samson Agonistes* is a war of opposites in which tension is increased as the opponents become progressively indistinguishable. This process begins in the encounter between Samson and the Chorus, the point of greatest difference and least tension, and culminates in the violence of Samson facing Harapha, mirror images of each other.[5] A literal reading of the play strongly suggests that it is Samson, and no one else, who is responsible for the increase of violence. His anger with himself, his disgust over his 'effeminate' weakness, at the beginning of the play is projected towards others as the action develops. Samson's anger is all-encompassing, and progressively contaminates the action. At the beginning of Dalila's scene, we find her aware of the danger she runs in exposing herself to Samson's violence: 'With doubtful feet and wavering resolution / I came, still dreading thy displeasure, Samson' (732–3). At the end of the interview, Dalila, having failed in her purpose as she suspected she would, underscores again the basis of their misunderstanding: 'Thy anger, unappeasable, still rages, / Eternal tempest never to be calmed' (963–4). Samson has an image of Dalila similar to that of the Chorus and Manoa prior to the interview, and the force of the interview is that it has the effect of transforming Dalila into this image. The ranting and unregenerate Dalila given us at the end of her scene is literally Samson's creation, in the image of himself; no one can escape from his vindictiveness and from his legendary

[5] See Girard, 'Symétrie', pp. 97–135, for his analysis of the structure of Greek drama in relation to its mythic intention.

violence. Everywhere he goes Samson ultimately encounters himself. His anger with others for having betrayed him is, as we know, simply an extension of the disgust he feels for his own actions. By the time he meets Harapha, Samson has been transported by his anger to such an extent that he is beside himself with rage; he has created his own self-caricature, and we immediately meet his parodic double in the person of Harapha.

The critical consensus has been particularly partial in its estimate of these interviews, noticing, to the exclusion of any ambiguity that the interviews serve to manifest the limitations of Dalila and Harapha. This, naturally, is the Chorus's conclusion: 'She's gone—a manifest serpent by her sting / Discovered in the end, till now concealed' (997–8). And with Harapha: 'His giantship is gone somewhat crestfallen' (1244). The parody is clear but it does not end with the rejection of Philistine virtue. For the irony is that, transported by his anger, Samson becomes no different from those he detests. Having defined himself as a fool in his first speech of the play, Samson, in his meeting with Harapha, illustrates that he had not been wrong in his estimate: 'The way to know were not to see, but taste' (1091). The difference now is that he is no longer aware of his limitations. Harapha's purpose, like that of Dalila, is reconciliation, but his good intentions are also subverted by Samson's violence. The overtones of Samson's rejections are more encompassing, however, in that Samson's violence is a contamination of the things which Dalila and Harapha represent: concepts of religious and secular order. In rejecting Dalila, Samson rejects her gods and the false priests who had counselled her; the rejection of Harapha includes the subversion of his gods and his secular chivalric code. Order of any kind is threatened by the violence of the play exemplified by Samson: he subverts the values maintained by the others. If order is no longer to be found in the world, the play, nevertheless, maintains its own logic and proportions; briefly, it evolves, despite the partisanship of the characters caught up in the action, its own 'fearful symmetry'.[6]

6 In the Prologue to the play, Milton phrases this movement to internal proportions, an action which is meant to be purgative, in medical terms: 'For so in psychic, things of melancholy hue and quality are used against melancholy, sour against sour, salt to remove salt humour.'

The same unbearable symmetry is found in *Paradise Lost* on the second day of the 'War in Heaven'. Solution to this conflict will require the intervention of Christ. Similarly, the tension in *Samson Agonistes* is relieved through an external agent, the Officer who bids Samson attend the feast of Dagon. The function of Christ and the Officer is to conclude the action through the expulsion of the agent responsible for the conflict. In this way, necessary differentiations are reintroduced into the epic and the play, and importantly, good can be distinguished from bad.

(iii) Discontinuity of language

In *Paradise Lost*, the delineation of good from evil is dealt with directly in terms of the poem's epic context and characterizations. But it is essential to see that Christ's role in the 'War in Heaven' is parallel to his creative function in Book VII. That is, in both mythological contexts, the Homeric 'war of the gods' and the creation story of Genesis, Christ has a single function and one which can only be approached in terms of his nature as divine *imago*, the living Word.

The Son fulfils the Father's words. Insofar as the Father's speech is enigmatic and demands interpretation, being an expression of immutable laws and, in this sense, closed in upon itself, the Son will draw out the Father's meaning in articulating what the Father leaves unsaid. Linguistically, the Son's mercy is nothing other than discursiveness. The properties of the Son's discursiveness are many, but for our purposes it is only necessary to single out his nature as one who articulates. If we look to Genesis, we find that the Word there also articulates and that this means separation. Articulation, distinction, separation: these are the antidotes to Chaos as found in Genesis and, more particularly, in *Paradise Lost*. 'Fluent speech' is the mark of the Son as 'Divine Similitude' and, in this capacity, he is able to distinguish not only words of doom from the words of comfort but good angels from bad, light from dark, and man from woman in Books VI and VII of the epic. At the end of the epic, Christ's mediatory nature becomes even more explicit as he is shown to be the only one capable of transforming the fallen and muddled speech of Adam into the acceptable dis-

course of prayer. As a fallen creature, Adam needs someone to
speak for him, to make sense of his nonsense, and to voice
his mute appeals for regeneration.

Samson, a fallen creature in need of intercession (one recalls
Milton's first analogy after the fall in *Paradise Lost* to Samson's
condition as we find him in the play, IX, 1059–62), finds himself in a far more ambiguous position. Like Adam before the
fall, Samson, prior to the play, was a 'Divine Similitude', a
manifestation of God's word and will, an indispensable link
in the 'Great Chain of Being', and it was in this way that he
understood himself as one who lived in the light: 'Promise was
that I / Should Israel from Philistine yoke deliver' (38–9).
His spiritual and symbolic reading of the world extended to the
most insignificant things: 'How slight the gift was, hung in my
hair' (59). Having betrayed his gift, his ability to see the world
as God's revelation, he interprets his change as extending to
the world's 'various objects of delight' (71). If the pre-fallen
existence of Samson is based on a direct access to divine revelation as mirrored in God's creation or communicated by an
angelic messenger, then the condition of the play is its opposite.
Samson's problems at the beginning of the play stem largely
from the failure of language to hold its meaning:..

> Your coming, friends, revives me; for I learn
> Now of my own experience, not by talk,
> How counterfeit a coin they are who 'friends'
> Bear in their superscription (of the most
> I would be understood).
>
> (187–91)

Language, for Samson, has become a matter of arbitrary associations, and it becomes this for others as the play proceeds.
Dalila, for instance, can say after her failure with Samson:
'Fame, if not double-faced, is double-mouthed, / And with contrary blast proclaims most deeds' (971–2). Of all the characters,
however, it is only Samson who seizes on the apocalyptic
dimensions of this loss of effective speech and who realizes
that there is no going back to a more comfortable time, an
option emphatically offered by Manoa, where signification was
still reliable. Samson's violence, a violence which undermines
the aspirations and convictions of others, is grounded in the

violence of his speech. Like the 'War in Heaven' in *Paradise Lost*, where the actual warfare of the angels is interspersed with invectives, each side hurling insults at the other in the same way that they eventually tear up the ground and hurl mountains, the warfare in *Samson Agonistes* is a battle of 'wits'. Language, for all intents and purposes, has become insult, polemic—in short, literary warfare. Samson, who was traditionally thought a riddler as expressed in the play, has become words without deeds, his own proper riddle which all the characters try to unravel.

Even the staging of the play enforces the interpretation of Samson's contradictory nature. Our first-hand knowledge of Samson, what is given directly through the action of the play, is of an all too human and feeble individual. Countering this weak image is the Samson of legend. We also know him through the play, but always through an intermediary. Samson's strength is never directly presented; rather, it is always re-presented through the other main characters or through the messenger at the end of the play.

Following Michel Foucault in *Les Mots et Les Choses* in his discussion of seventeenth-century language, it is possible to interpret the structure of re-presentation in *Samson Agonistes* as the conversion of the 'real' Samson into a pure sign 'which is good to think with'.[7] There are many indications of this in the play, and most of them are voiced by the Chorus, considering it is the Chorus which is ordinarily prone to see Samson as a symbol of Israel's deliverance. Most importantly, however, it is Samson who must come to see himself as a sign and, in this sense, as the source of his own re-presentability. Like Christ in *Paradise Lost* whose function is to 'actualize' himself as *logos*, Samson's task is to become what he was intended to be for all time: a sign for others who through him can achieve salvation. The role of the hero requires that he become an individual, different from others as the function of *logos* is differentiation and distinctiveness if it is to carry any meaning.

As a sign, following Foucault's analysis of Baroque semiology, the weak Samson relates to the strong Samson as signifier

---

[7] *Les Mots et Les Choses* (Paris, 1966), pp. 72–81. A more general approach to the problem is suggested by Claude Lévi-Strauss' discussion of the symbolic function of totemism in *The Savage Mind*, pp. 104–8.

to signified. Samson will remain indecisive so long as he fails
to recognize his paradoxical nature as symbol to a people. He
must come to recognize that his function is purely ritualistic
as he does in the theatre at Gaza, and that his beneficial role
for a people, contrary to his earlier thoughts, is to be 'in
power of others, never in my own' (78).

The recurring image in the play which best expresses Samson's
divided character and the symbolic function he is meant to
serve is that of God's fool.[8] In the first speech, he characterizes
himself 'still as a fool' (77); later, with the Chorus, he says:

> To have revealed
> Secrets of men, the secrets of a friend,
> How heinous had the fact been how deserving
> Contempt and scorn of all—to be excluded
> All friendship, and avoided as a blab,
> The mark of fool set on his front!
>
> (491–6)

Manoa and Dalila have no trouble convincing him that he
was foolish in love, but what finally bothers Samson most is
the presumption of the Philistines:

> Can they think me so broken, so debased
> With corporal servitude, that my mind ever
> Will condescend to such absurd commands?
> Although their drudge, to be their fool or jester.
>
> (1335–8)

Yet, it is always his foolishness which is caused by 'divine
impulsion prompting' (422) or some 'rousing motions' (1382).
In both his foolish marriages and his performance at the
'spacious theatre' of Gaza, Samson is prompted and, in both
instances the purpose is the same: the rejection of cultural
differences and the myths which nurture this difference.

Although the theatre to Milton's time had traditionally
served as a 'mirror of our fickle state' in a mimetic presentation
of a pre-existing order, in Samson Agonistes it posits its own order

[8] Arnold Stein, *Heroic Knowledge* (Hamdon, Connecticut: Archon Books, 1965), p. 196.

out of a disordered world. The fact that Samson in his last action destroys a theatre 'with seats where all the lords, and each degree / Of sort, might sit in order to behold' (1607–8), and that when the theatre is destroyed 'the vulgar only scaped, who stood without' (1659), indicates that the fundamental irony of the spectacle is directed toward the false resemblances of order and hierarchical structure in the 'real' world.

(iv) Medicine man

Anthropological sources teach us that Samson's behaviour is not unusual either from the point of view of primitive ritual or myth; the Chorus also emphasizes Samson's typical nature in terms of the myth of the book of Judges (277–89). In an article which deals with numerous examples of the ritual clown and the trickster figure in primitive societies, Laura Makarius argues that the clown's function is to violate the taboos of his tribe. Like Samson, the primitive clown is both dangerous and beneficial, as Mrs Makarius says: dangerous in the violation of taboos and beneficial in that he 'invokes the violation, hypostasized in myth' in order to get 'good medicine'. This ambivalence dictates the fact that he 'must be kept at a distance'.[9] For the same reason, Samson's challenge is refused by Harapha in fear that he will be contaminated (1106–7), and more generally, Samson's last action as a fool is set off at a distance in Gaza.

Samson is a sacred fool, and his role in this capacity is to break the taboos of his tribe. Obviously, his marriages to women outside his tribe is intended to underscore this function, and none of his 'friends' miss a chance to remind him of this fact. Another violation, however, the manner of his death among the Philistines, is not faced as squarely. Hearing of Samson's death from the Messenger, Manoa's first impulse is to seize on the problematical nature of this event:

Messenger: Unwounded of his enemies he fell.
Manoa: Wearied with slaughter, then, or how? explain.
Messenger: By his own hands.

[9] 'Ritual Clown and Symbolic Behaviour', *Diogenes*, 69 (1970), pp. 46, 56.

> *Manoa:*   Self-violence! What cause
> Brought him so soon at variance with himself
> Among his foes?
>
>   (1582–7)

The problem of Samson's suicide gives rise to a great deal of equivocation by the Chorus, but it is never resolved. This interchange between Manoa and the Messenger, however, is certainly intended to record the fact that in his death Samson has committed yet another tribal violation. Manoa and the Chorus are saved the ordeal of solving this riddle in falling on the Philistines as scapegoats. As the Semichorus summarizes:

> While their hearts were jocund and sublime,
> Drunk with idolatry, drunk with wine
> And fat regorged of bulls and goats,
> Chaunting their idol, and preferring
> Before our living Dread, who dwells
> In Silo, his bright sanctuary.
> Among them he a spirit of frenzy sent,
> Who hurt their minds,
> And urged them on with mad desire
> To call in haste for their destroyer.
>
>   (1669–78)

These are comforting words because the Chorus fails to appreciate the extent of the loss. The House of Dan has lost its deliverer in the holocaust; as we know from the Old Testament, their lineage ends with Samson. The redemptive line, at the end of the book of Judges, is transferred to a female Gentile, Ruth, and it is she who ushers in the triumphant line of David and the last deliverer, Christ. That the Chorus and Manoa are able to transfer their culpability to the Philistines means very little in terms of the Messianic line. Nevertheless, it tells us a great deal about the final comfort of the play.

Manoa, having been cheered by the good news, conceives of erecting a monument to commemorate Samson's achievement:

> There will I build him
> A monument, and plant it round with shade

Of laurel ever green and branching palm,
With all his trophies hung, and acts enrolled
In copious legend, or sweet lyric song.
Thither shall all the valiant youth resort,
And from his memory inflame their breasts
To matchless valour and adventures high;
The virgins also shall, on feastful days,
Visit his tomb with flowers, only bewailing
His lot unfortunate in nuptial choice,
From whence captivity and loss of eyes.

(1733-44)

Plainly, Manoa's purpose is to turn Samson into an idol, to be visited on 'feastful days'. In addition, the monument will encourage the youth of his tribe to imitate Samson's behaviour. In short, Manoa's purpose, profoundly ironic in this respect, is to transform his people into the image of the Philistines: idol worshippers and warriors. He has failed to learn his lesson, as have the members of the Chorus, and what he suggests is only more of the same. This is especially disturbing when we realize that violence toward others, as Samson has shown, is ultimately self-violence.

Rather than serving as an incentive to martial behaviour, Samson's purpose is to illustrate the futility of inter-tribal strife. As an agent of the 'sacred', Samson's function is to convince all those who 'have the eyes to see' that power of any kind is the prerogative of God and not something to be easily appropriated by his people. Insofar as the God of the play is a 'living Dread', sacrilege is nothing else than the usurpation of the 'Thunderer's' power; it is a state of pollution and violence. As René Girard has said with respect to *Oedipus Rex*, it is the condition of the plague.[10] Violence ends when men, no longer thinking themselves gods in their usurpation of power, acknowledge the true and single God. Thus it is to be 'separate to God'. For in acknowledging this truth, Samson marries women from outside his group, suggesting in this way the similarity of the tribes and the possibility of Christian brotherhood. That Manoa and the Chorus, not to mention the Philistines, fail to see this as Samson's truth is indicative that their allegiance is to

10 'Symétrie', p. 112.

a violent code. They will always discover contradictions and oppositions where similarity exists.

Finally, Samson's tribe is no different from the Philistines when 'Sacrifice / Had fill'd thir hearts with mirth, high cheer, and wine' (1612–13), insofar as Manoa and the Chorus are overjoyed with the outcome of the action, an action which has transformed the Philistines into a sacrificial offering to the vengeful God of the Israelites. In terms of Samson's encounter with his antagonists, and to the extent that the two groups experience their fundamental similarity as difference, the basic difference of good and evil, they illustrate the nature of the myth which they put into practice as not only constituting an illusory difference, but as creating its own misconception. Samson, at the root of the myth being enacted by the play, is one who 'with amaze shall strike all who behold' (1645). That Samson's last act is misunderstood is indicative that the myth has done its work in creating a mask (Samson as fool), veiling its true function as an instrument of violence. Thus, it is the myth which is the final source of doubleness in the play and which demands demystification because it is presented as a God-given intrusion in human affairs in the form of the miraculous event at Gaza, a miracle which is interpreted significantly as a sign of God's perpetual covenant with the Israelites.

But Samson can be said to be in possession of the truth, like Christ, only insofar as 'the vulgar who stood without' are unaware of the real significance of his last action and of the nature of his strength which is not derived from 'above' through divine intercession and illumination. Rather, Samson, at the end of his career, is very much like Christ in *Paradise Regained*, knowing that he has been called, but in the dark concerning the specific mission he must undertake. His patience at this point contrasts with his impatience throughout most of the play, first with himself and, then, with those who come to see him; he has come to realize that he must wait on the fullness of time and that his actions have meaning in another time than his own. With this realization follows the destruction of all he had stood for up to this point, particularly, the destruction of his earlier conception of his role as hero.

Samson begins the play by lamenting his loss of heroism and relives a past where he shined as God's anointed hero, and it is some time later before he realizes that his true heroic stature depends on his stand against the very heroism which had sustained him in the past. He must destroy himself as hero, must shatter the icon he has become for himself as for others, must destroy and pull down the 'two massy Pillars' of the temple in which he venerates his own righteousness and strength. The movement is from idol and idol-worshipper to iconoclast.

Samson accepts the role of fool at the end, because he wishes to underline the nature of his earlier heroism, that he had always been a fool in his stance as hero—all the more so for his unconscious acceptance of his role. To act the fool consciously, however, is not only to point to his previous blindness but to transcend his earlier status. Moreover, as fool, Samson detracts from everything which is deep, profound, mystifying, and miraculous. In contradistinction to the operations of myths, he emphasizes that the truth is not 'out-there' but 'here' on the surface for all to see, a truth, in short, available to the 'lowly wise' which can transform weakness into strength.

9
The plainness of
Paradise Regained:
unmaking 'strange'

It was subtle of God to learn Greek when he wished to become an author—and not learn it better.

Nietzsche, *Beyond Good and Evil*

When we have to change our mind about a person, we hold the inconvenience he causes us very much against him.

Nietzsche, *Beyond Good and Evil*

If *Paradise Lost* is intended to 'see and tell / Of things invisible to mortal sight,' *Paradise Regained* inverts this formula.[1] Milton's short epic deals exclusively with what can be seen in the concrete reality surrounding Christ's earthly mission. Similarly, in *Samson Agonistes*, the hero, the true hero, learns that the meaning of his life is not obscure, except when he avoids the obvious: Samson's meaning lies before him if only he has the courage to accept it. Samson had always been headed in a single direction because his life was a living testimony to the contradictions inherent in a violent code.

Samson eventually encounters his malignant double and comes to terms with the blindness he had lamented at the beginning of the play, once he acknowledges that the obstacles, doubleness and blindness, were of his own making. While imprisoned at Gaza, he thinks that his condition is the result of the deceptions of others and he is only sporadically aware

[1] *Cf.* William B. Hunter, Jnr, 'The Obedience of Christ in *Paradise Regained*', *Calm of Mind*, ed. Joseph Wittreich, Jnr (Cleveland: Case Western Reserve University Press, 1971), p. 67.

of the extent to which he forges his own chains. Seeing this
at last, the obstacles disappear and the way which had been
closed is opened. In other words, while Samson is unwilling
to recognize his past as anything more than a series of failures
resulting from the deceptions of others, his life seems meaningless to him; no further action is of any use. This explains his
curious inactivity at the start of the play. But as his life passes
before him in the series of encounters which make up the play,
he grasps the range of meanings which he represents for others,
from deliverer of Israel to son and husband and his status,
finally, as hero. For others, at least, his life is significant and
they take every opportunity to interpret Samson as a comforting
sign. Samson's heroism is for them a primary obstacle, since it
appears as a response to a higher calling, a more encompassing
destiny, and, equally, this heroism allows Samson to see himself
in a favourable light because it overshadows his other contradictory roles. Heroism is discontinuous with other earthly
callings as the sign of a strength more than human which transforms the merely human into insignificance.

But the Samson seen in the play has lost his heroic character,
and this loss places him in a particularly vulnerable position
in that it makes a mockery of his earlier achievements and
transforms him into a fool. Once the rationalizations attendant on a heroic stance are taken from Samson, he grasps that
his life until this time had fed on an illusory strength, a strength
which required the repression of the contradictory nature of his
roles and the vanity of his motivation. Heroism, in other words,
offers him the opportunity to hide from himself, from his
perplexing history, and his recovery demands that he face these
contradictions and come to terms with his riddling nature.

Consequently, he rejects his father as representative of the
double bind in which he finds himself, because it is the father's
allegiance to tribal law which demands unswerving obedience
from the son in fulfilling the father's desire for retribution.
For the father, Manoa, is the earthly prototype of the Old
Testament God, the 'living Dread' who is 'justified' at the end
of the play. Whether Samson is conscious of this is unclear.
To rephrase the issue, it could be argued that Samson, in his
last days, accepts the father—he will follow the laws of his
tribe—where, earlier, he had set himself against Manoa in his

marriages. But to follow the father in this case does not necessarily mean to imitate his wrath; rather, it is to see bondage to the father's ways as the only source of liberation.

Manoa is treated ironically at the end of the play and shown returning from his bartering with the Philistines only to find his son gone. Manoa is left in the dark, but not Samson, who discovers the true father as light in darkness, hope in despair, and wisdom in folly. Equally, in giving up the father, Samson rejects his faith in origins, the promise that the spirit and letter of the law come together in heroic actions meant to deliver the Israelites. He learns that his faith in his own origin, his belief in his invincibility as God's anointed, is one with the heroic strength he possesses in his hair: a miraculous interpretation at best. Samson rejects the interpretation (we recall how little he has to say about the 'intimate impulse' which leads him to the theatre at Gaza), when he realizes that it has no value in itself, but is always dependent on the person who speaks the words. The miraculous interpretation of his birth, for instance, depends on the knowledge that it is the product of a tyrannized people, projecting its desire for independence onto a sacred birth which will vindicate them. Specifically, in terms of the play, interpretation is always the result of the interpreter's judgement on a previous speaker. Dalila is wrong in what she says, not because her argument is necessarily fallacious—it seems plausible from one point of view—but because she is the one who frames the speeches. She has been proved false once before; consequently, whatever she may now say is tainted by her previous guilt. Thus, interpretation is little more than the determination of guilt. This Samson discovers as he tries to interpret his past. Ultimately, his interpretation leads back to his own guilt and his personal responsibility for his imprisonment. From this fact, one which Samson begins with in the play, it is an easy step to the awareness that interpretation is accusation and that every accusation calls up its own double in the form of a counter-accusation creating an objective situation where the accuser is no better than the one he accuses.

All of this is on the surface of the play. It might represent, for that matter, the very structure of theatre as Milton understood it: a series of dramatic oppositions which are, in reality, not oppositions, except as they engage the fantasies of the spectators and actors, another meaning, perhaps, of the theatre as a 'mirror of our fickle state' with the emphasis on the doubling and illusory nature of the mirror as medium. As mirror, the theatre is experienced as depth, profundity: something 'beyond' which sustains the wavering action of the surface. All we have, however, is the mirror, an illusory depth with nothing but surface. Mirrors are read in reverse; where we find doubt, we should read certainty; for the wavering line, firmness; and so forth. Therefore, the apparently haphazard events which constitute Samson's life are only meaningless and hazy if seen through a glass darkly, for we find him at the end appreciative of the fact that he will not swerve from the law of his fathers, which, interpreted by the Chorus means one thing, but from our point of view, means that his life, like his ending, will be lawful because it is intelligible. His paradoxical ending simply points to the contradictory nature of the law he will fulfil, and, in this sense, it is perfectly intelligible and lawful. As his life had been a response to the contradictions of the law, so his death brings the law full circle: an ending perfectly consistent with its origin in the realization that his freedom demands a full acceptance of the *binding* nature of law on actions which he had felt were somehow free of restraint. Law, then, as a principle of intelligibility means structure where no structure seems to exist and meaning where everything gives the impression of insignificance. The law is no hidden cause or inexplicable phenomena; rather, it exhibits itself on the surface in the apparent inconsistencies of everyday life. Law, in short, is the intelligibility of the surface structure, the source of all meaning which is not intended to mystify and 'amaze'.[2]

In *Paradise Regained*, Christ's purpose is to show through his concrete actions the intelligibility of the law. The fact that Satan can offer Christ in his temptations the bounty of the earth should not deter the critic from acknowledging that Satan's abundance can be reduced to a single law. Satan rules the earth and possesses everything in it, and this he gives Christ to see in the temptations, but what appears as the variety and

[2] See Lévi-Strauss' introduction to Marcel Mauss, *Sociologie et Anthropologie* (Paris: Presses Universitaires de France, 1950), pp. xxviii, xxxvii.

abundance of this show can be reduced to a basic observation
that it rests on the distortions of 'air', the specific element which
separates Satan from God. Air as incipient speech, and also air
as the medium through which the 'strange Parallax or Optic
skill / Of vision multiplied through air' (IV, 40–41) works its
magic in transforming what is close and intimate into the
strange and distant. And it is this strangeness created by distance which gives the illusion of difference where, in fact,
everything is the same.

More particularly, the temptations concern the re-making
of Christ into something other than he is, a man of humble
origins lost in a 'woody maze' (II, 246). Satan would have
Christ show his difference from all others either through his
power delegated by God or in ascribing to the devil's policy
which he is promised will transform him into a god among men.
In offering Christ the opportunity to be different, Satan exemplifies that all difference is arbitrary and unintelligible. To be a
great warrior, king, or sage matters little, so long as one is
different, among the first rank and great among men. For
Christ, it comes down to the question of fame and the fickleness
of the multitudes who value fame only to pass on to someone
else, once a hero's ascendancy begins to ebb:

> For what is glory but the blaze of fame,
> The people's praise, if always praise unmixt?
> And what the people but a herd confus'd,
> A miscellaneous rabble, who extol
> Things vulgar, and well weigh'd, scarce worth the praise?
> They praise and they admire they know not what;
> And know not whom, but as one leads the other;
> And what delight to be by such extoll'd,
> To live upon thir tongues and be thir talk,
> Of whom to be disprais'd were no small praise?
> His lot who dares be singularly good.
> Th'intelligent among them and the wise
> Are few, and glory scarce of few is rais'd.
> This is true glory and renown, when God
> Looking on th'Earth, with approbation marks
> The just man, . . .
>
> (III, 47–62)

To the multitude all heroes are the same, and, of course, the judgement is correct even though 'they know not what' they mean. Equally, Satan is absolutely right in his last indignant retort to Christ, even though he completely misunderstands his own truth:

> I thought thee worth my nearer view
> And narrower Scrutiny, that I might learn
> In what degree or meaning thou art call'd
> The Son of God, which bears no single sense;
> The Son of God I also am, or was,
> And if I was, I am; relation stands;
> All men are Sons of God; yet thee I thought
> In some respect far higher so declar'd.
>
> And opportunity I here have had
> To try thee, sift thee, and confess have found thee
> Proof against all temptation as a rock
> Of Adamant, and as a Center, firm;
> To th'utmost of mere man both wise and good,
> Not more; for Honors, Riches, Kingdoms, Glory
> Have been before contemn'd, and may again:

(IV, 514-37)

As 'Son of God', Christ is similar to all men and defeats Satan from this precise vantage point: he defeats Satan through his similarity and not his difference to all men. Any other method would imply his subjugation to Satan's snares which are based on a surreptitious difference, because it is arbitrary and meaningless.

Satan's problem is that he persists in interpreting the expression 'Son of God', since in his judgement it 'bears no single meaning'. Christ, by contrast, posits that the phrase has only one meaning, that everyone is a 'Son of God' while 'relation stands'. To think otherwise is to maintain one's difference from others and, in this stance, to sacrifice the 'other' to vindicate oneself as true 'Son of God'. Thus, it is the literal sense which bears the meaning in *Paradise Regained*, insofar as the literal sense bears on the law. Yet, Satan's sarcasm demands a response:

A Kingdom they portend thee, but what Kingdom,
Real or Allegoric I discern not,
Nor when, eternal sure, as without end,
Without beginning; for no date prefixt
Directs me in the Starry Rubric set.

(IV, 389–93)

Christ's Kingdom is not of this world; this does not mean that it is not real, nor does it mean that the kingdom is of another world (allegoric), if we conceive of other world as a place. Rather, as the reader is told in the invocation to Book I, Christ's kingdom is the 'Paradise within' promised at the end of *Paradise Lost*. To be a 'real' kingdom, like Parthia, would require that it come under the rule of Satan, and to be 'allegoric' would mean for Christ to give up his earthly mission as man, these two interpretations constituting the poles of the Satanic temptations. In effect, the temptations are much the same: the former, stipulating Christ's difference on earth and the latter, a substitution of an ineffectual earthly difference by the miraculous interposition of a god-like difference, which is little more than a projection of man's impotence against the wiles of Satan.

Christ's method is to undercut this illusory difference, and the manner in which he is able to do this is simply by being a better historian than Satan. Whenever Satan generalizes the advantages which he can offer Christ, whether 'Honors, Riches, Kingdoms, Glory', Christ responds in either of two ways. First, and this is the least interesting tack, although pertinent in terms of the earlier discussion of the roots of interpretation in the 'who', he invariably emphasizes the Satanic source of the words being spoken to him ('Knowing who I am, as I know who thou art' (I, 356), and, in addition, he maintains that what seems advantageous may mask far greater misfortunes: 'A Crown, / Golden in show, is but a wreath of thorns' (II, 458–9). To counteract Satan's tendency of relying on the most immediate and easy interpretation of generalities, Christ uses his most potent instrument which is nothing else than discernment. He counters Satan's generalities with the concrete facts gleaned from his study of history and observation of those around him who could be said to possess

'Honors, Riches, Kingdoms, Glory'. All these advantages are finally shown to be, in terms of the specifics upon which they are grounded, more the source of hardship than happiness.

Satan hits on the crucial difference between his method and Christ's when he suggests:

> Hard are the ways of truth, and rough to walk
> Smooth on the tongue discourst, pleasing to th'ear,
> And tunable as Silvan Pipe or Song;
>
> (I, 479–81)

Rhetorically, Satan is a sophist, as many have noticed with respect to his stance in *Paradise Lost*. Christ, on the other hand, is a philologist, or, in Nietzsche's framework, a genealogist: he goes to the roots of words as founded upon concrete events.[3] In uncovering the specific origin of 'soothing words', Christ shows that these words are masks for concrete historical events which, if truly named, would command no admiration. For the history of these words is written in blood and the unlawful domination of one group by another. Abstractions require blood sacrifice, the sanction of all domination.

Christ is equally demanding with respect to his own history. The poem begins with his proclamation; originally, 'obscure, / Unmarkt, unknown' (I, 24–5), he comes for baptism at the hands of the 'Great Proclaimer' (18), and a sign descends from above. His temptation, not that which Satan creates, concerns his understanding of this sign. Characteristically, he seeks understanding by reviewing his own proper history and resists throughout the temptation to abstract the concrete nature of his earthly mission. To do so would imply the transformation of his sign into a miraculous dispensation from above in neglecting his own history. He has entertained the possibility of miraculously influencing his followers, but he resists this temptation by awaiting a further sign. This is the basis of Christ's technique: 'Thought following thought, and step by step led on' (I, 192). His faithfulness to this procedure, 'step by step', initially creates an internal lack of composure:

> O what a multitude of thoughts at once
> Awak'n'd in me swarm, while I consider

[3]*Cf*. Nietzsche, *The Genealogy of Morals*.

> What from within I feel myself, and hear
> What from without comes often to my ears,
> Ill sorting with my present state compar'd.
>
> (I, 196–200)

Christ has been proclaimed; the sign has been given. Yet, exactly at this juncture where one would expect his acceptance of the prerogatives of regal power, he discovers an inconsistency.[4] The outside and inside are discontinuous because his thoughts suggest great deeds while around him he sees a desert not in keeping with his inner persuasion. But he does attune himself to the outside in 'thought following thought', because, in the dialectic process, each thought is the deconstruction of the previous one; dialectically, it is the destruction of idols, since no thought or perception is allowed to be superior over the others. In this way, he duplicates his wandering in the wilderness by mirroring internally the images of waste and solitude which surround him. This it is to be led on by something other than the Satanic voice forever promising instant solutions and miraculous interventions.

Christ's method is the model for Milton's activity in the poem:

> Thou Spirit who led'st this glorious Eremite
> Into the Desert, his Victorious Field
> Against the Spiritual Foe, and brought'st him thence
> By proof th'undoubted Son of God, inspire,
> As thou are wont, my prompted Song, else mute,
> And bear through height or depth of nature's bounds
> With prosperous wing full summ'd to tell of deeds
> Above Heroic, though in secret done,
> And unrecorded left through many an Age,
> Worthy t' have not remain'd so long unsung.
>
> (I, 8–17)

The parallel with Christ is obvious: what needs emphasis, however, is Milton's technique of 'proving' Christ's divinity 'above Heroic' through his manhood. The method is one of

---

[4] The disciples and Mary also experience this dichotomy at the beginning of Book II.

inversion; as the Satanic is defeated by showing that the pre-
tension to godhead is founded on the particular repression of
what is human in this desire, so true divinity requires the
repression of all desire for godhead in an emphasis on what is
truly human without the aid of divine intercession. The question
of obedience, stressed in the invocation, simply emphasizes the
necessity to find one's salvation as man, not as a god. As well,
it indicates that to be obedient is to remain human and not
attempt to assume God's prerogatives.

In being obedient, one might expect immediate rewards as
a confirmation of the faith one has put in God's providence.
At the very least, one might expect happiness. It may well be,
however, that happiness is the final obstacle to the faithful.
To achieve happiness, all is given, everything is sacrificed,
and invariably, one finds at that moment when this last abstrac-
tion seems attainable—through a side-long glance over which
there is no control—the price that must be paid for this temporary fixation, the past which must be forgotten if the fruits of
the labour are to be enjoyed. Is it any accident that these
expectations are transformed into a pillar of salt?

In both *Paradise Regained* and *Paradise Lost*, the overall
impression is gloomy: the fall signals the loss of everything and,
most of all, it means the end of happiness. Christ and Mary
might be expected to possess the 'Paradise within', but what
this means in practical terms is pain and suffering: 'A Crown, /
Golden in show, is but a wreath of thorns.' Consolation, in this
context, is a dream, an illusory banquet, and a vindication not
forthcoming. Is it surprising that faced with this evidence,
rewards and happiness are sought in other worlds in the construction of an iron-clad Platonism which situates the form of
the 'good' elsewhere than on earth? This sublimation is dealt
with convincingly as Christ describes Plato as one who 'to
fabling fell and smooth conceits' (IV, 295) in attempting to
locate the 'good' outside this world.

Echoing Nietzsche, it can be said that the truth of *Paradise
Regained* is unpleasant and that the Platonic 'good' may not be
good for Milton. There are other truths than those which
comfort us, so Nietzsche implies when considering the English
psychologists of the seventeenth century—a group rarely men-
tioned in relation to Milton: they 'know how to keep their

hearts and their sufferings in bounds and have trained themselves to sacrifice all desirability to truth, *every* truth, even plain,
harsh, ugly, repellent, unchristian, immoral truth. . . . For such
truths do exist. . .'⁵ Nietzsche explains his fascination for this
group:

> These English psychologists—what do they really want?
> One always discovers them voluntarily or involuntarily at
> the same task, namely at dragging the *partie honteuse* of our
> inner world into the foreground and seeking the truly
> effective and directing agent, that which has been decisive
> in its evolution, in just that place where the intellectual pride
> of man would least *desire* to find it (in the *vis inertiae* of
> habit, for example, or in forgetfulness, or in a blind and
> chance mechanistic hooking-together of ideas, or in something
> purely passive, automatic, reflexive, molecular, and thor-
> oughly stupid)—what is it really that always drives these
> psychologists in just *this* direction?⁶

Applied to Christ, Nietzsche's statement shows that Christ's
mission concerns the rejection of the image of man fabricated
by the humanists of the Renaissance: man as an image of the
gods fully in control of his destiny. For this idol and ideal,
Paradise Regained substitutes the 'old man' of the first temptation,
controlled by habit, forgetfulness, and blind chance. Once
recognized, the old man shows himself as an earthly mask for
Satan, a creature who, in a word, has become stupid; stupid,
that is, to the extent that he has learned nothing new since his
initial rebellion.

Because of this ignorance, Satan, in *Paradise Regained*, is
constantly rehearsing his old ploys in a conventional theatre
which has lost the power to persuade since that time when it was
recognized as an illusion—pure artifice with little grounding in
facts. It is precisely Satan's readiness to re-work his habitual
temptations—they worked in the past—and his instinctive
response to Christ which finally betrays him. He is betrayed
at last by his own blindness and stupidity as he encounters an
agent 'above Heroic'. Caught up in a situation where the old

⁵ *The Genealogy of Morals*, First Essay, Section 1, p. 461.
⁶ Ibid., p. 460.

rules no longer apply, where he can no longer avoid a con-
frontation with the 'truth', he is dumbfounded and exasperated.
When his traditional disguises are taken away, he is left
defenceless, not knowing what to say or what to do. Nevertheless, he goes through the motions and underlines the hopelessness of his condition and the degree of his ignorance.

Forever in search of 'signs', forever creating narcissistic
signs which substantiate his possession of the earth, Satan is
left 'without sign of boast, or sign of joy, / Solicitous and
blank' (II, 119–20). In *Paradise Regained*, the sign is replaced
by the 'mark' which has no other reference than the body, as it
is the marked body in Book XI of *Paradise Lost* which designates
temperance or intemperance.[7] Satan is marked as the 'old
man', and we are led to see that the mark not only represents,
as the sign does, but is, as well, the particular creation of his
blindness and ignorance.

The mark, as opposed to the sign, is an unconscious creation
of Satan's life: it is what he has become for all to *see*. No
mystery here; simply the body as a written record of his
habits, desires, likes, and dislikes, in short, of the body as the
mark of his destiny. As the Prince of Air, Satan would have
Christ forget the body; he would persuade Christ to act as if
he had no body. Interestingly, his temptations concern the
hunger of the body, escape from the body through the devices
of Greek philosophy, and, finally, the temptation of the temple
involves overcoming the law of gravity, the property of bodies
to *fall* to the earth.

Satan, one way or another, tries to make Christ admit
through word or deed the separation of body and spirit, and,
as we know, the tension Christ feels between his internal state
and what surrounds him on the outside in his opening medita-
tion is also focused on the problem of body and spirit. But, for
Christ, the problem is only an apparent one, since his method is
to coordinate 'thought following thought' with 'step by step'
and achieve a condition similar to that of the angels circling
the throne of God: 'Singing, while the hand / Sung with the
voice' (I, 171–2).

[7] Michel Foucault developed this distinction in a lecture delivered in
1972 at the University of Montreal: 'Théâtre, Cérémonie et Politique au
XVIIᵉ Siècle'.

The metaphor, as in *Paradise Lost*, is that of the circle and the mirror, of Christ as the perfect image of God. But the circle is only meaningful if events are allowed to unravel in the 'fulness of time'. Any single point, miraculous or otherwise, extracted from the whole distorts the mirrored structure of *Paradise Regained* joined at both ends by the proclamations of St John the Baptist and the choir of angels. The circling hours must be experienced if their significance is to be manifested, if God's time is to be transformed into human time.

Yet, God's time is not continuous with human history; this is the point of Christ's meditations and those of Mary and his disciples. Divine meaning is always experienced as more, as a supplement, as something more added to man's life. As Christ says to Satan in the first temptation: 'Man lives not by Bread only, but each Word / Proceeding from the mouth of God, who fed / Our Fathers here with Manna' (I, 349–51). God's word is an interruption of the ordinary processes of history, or, more exactly, it represents a radical rupture which offers the opportunity of a new beginning. But as a new beginning, it is fraught with uncertainty, except as it is interpreted as a nostalgic return to old origins. This is why God's divine intercession in his proclamation is experienced by Christ as a movement into a mazy labyrinth of the desert, where chance (chance associations, encounters, thoughts) controls events. Thus, what we find is the substitution of the concept of history as an externalizing of human consciousness, of history as capable of control through a humanistic conception of man, by a concept of history as the interplay of presence and absence, a game of chance sporadically illuminated by the words of God—manna in the desert. In the words of Jacques Derrida, it is this realization which allows Christ to 'brush aside all the facts', to threat Satan's evidence, facts which had always been compelling in the past, with scorn. For, 'he must always conceive of the origin of a new structure on the model of catastrophe— an overturning of nature in nature, a natural interruption of a natural sequence, a brushing aside *of* nature',[8] and, we might add, an overturning of man's nature, conceived by the humanists, as capable of rationally determining its own history. Rather, in *Paradise Regained*, reason is the last temptation: it

---

[8] 'Structure, Sign, and Play,' in *The Languages of Criticism*, p. 263.

gives the impression of freeing man from the snares and de-
lusions of Satan, but only that he might bind one all the more
firmly to his pride and illusions.

It needs to be stressed that to doubt the efficacy of reason
is not necessarily to fall into unintelligibility. For, what is
suspicious are the pretensions associated with reason after it
has been acknowledged by 'the first and wisest of them all . . .
to know this only, that he nothing knew' (IV, 293-4). God's
reason differs from man's, and because of this, man experiences
God's truth as a rupture of history and as the undercutting
of his plans and reasons. God introduces chance into the world
and were it not for this all would be doomed. (Stated differently,
one could say that God respects the difference of the 'single
just man' and if Satan had his way, everyone would be the same,
doomed to his illusions and to his Hell.) Thus, it is in chance
that the operations of the spirit are discovered, not chance as
the pagan reading of the meaninglessness of life, but as a divine
interruption of man's ways.

Chance spells out the end of the tyranny of myths, of the
'*Theban* Monster' and his riddle as well as 'Earth's Son Antaeus'
who received 'from his mother Earth new strength, / Fresh
from his fall' (IV, 563-75). Myths, riddles, and ambiguous
words are replaced by plain words and deeds recorded in the
New Testament, though 'unrecorded left through many an
Age'.

History and beyond

'In your labyrinth there are three lines too many,' he said at last. 'I know of one Greek labyrinth which is a single straight line. Along that line so many philosophers have lost themselves that a mere detective might well do so, too. . . .'

Borges, 'Death and the Compass'

Each of Milton's major poems stages temptations and these temptations lead to the creation of a responsible, moral being, the 'single just man' of *Paradise Lost*. As *Paradise Lost* maintains, 'reason is choice', and temptations are given in order to exercise reason. But the purpose is more than an academic and isolated testing of the attributes of reason, because, as choice, reason is engagement. Reason enters the arena of chance in the engagement of choice, and, 'at stake' in this context, is reason itself, the particular 'reason' for the experience. In other words, the 'single just man' does not stand in isolation; he can never merely stand against the world or against the laws of nations, even though we learn in *Paradise Regained* that 'Nations' remain under Satan's sway and express his continuing influence over human affairs. Rather the moral agent, often characterized by Milton as a prophet, represents a textual development and continuation. Without his choice, there is no future and no movement, but only the unstable present of equivocations, of choices not taken. To fail to choose is to be bound to the past, to be overcome by past mistakes: it is to be a captive of history.

Choice is a closure and an opening. It reveals history as redundancy and the debilitating destiny of a present which is finalized in its passing. Equally, choice reveals 'of his steps the track Divine' (XI, 354), a passage through time and the forging of an individual conscience and purpose through the

present as an opening in time. Consequently, it is more than a
question of determining the moral integrity of the prophet as
one who stands apart and decries the degenerate ways of
nations. The prophet is also an instrument of cultural transformations:

> Him on this *Euphrates* yet residing
> Bred up in Idol-worship; O that men
> (Canst thou believe?) should be so stupid grown,
> While yet the Patriarch liv'd who scap'd the Flood,
> As to forsake the living God, and fall
> To worship their own work in Wood and Stone
> For Gods! yet him God the most high voutsafes
> To call by Vision from his Father's house,
> His kindred and false Gods, into a Land
> Which he will show him, and from him will raise
> A mighty Nation, . . .
>
> (XII, 114–24)

This passage depicts two forms of history. The first, and the
one rejected by Abraham, is the past and, more specifically,
the past as it controls the present since it is directed to human
culture and those images which perpetuate man's enslavement
to his forms and insure that history will include nothing which
is not of man's own making. For this reason, it is a closed and
visible history. The alternative to this monumental (in the
erection of idols) and visible history is 'to call by vision', using
history as a way out of history. This second history, in the
fabric of *Paradise Lost*, is to know good from evil, but, more
importantly, it is to see good arising out of evil. It is to understand the history of man as more than a response to a human
voice and the externalizing of man's desire for recognition.

Similarly, in *Paradise Regained*, Christ is presented with a
series of temptations which are understandable in terms of the
arena in which they are staged. Again, the context and rationale
of temptations is history. History, then, is the final temptation:
it is the ultimate labyrinth in which man 'amazes' himself.
In this logic, salvation means the end of history, particularly
if it represents and makes visible human conflict and struggles
for domination recorded in a visible history. For this reason,

Paradise Regained, as a record of temptations overcome, is an overcoming of history.

> . . . though in secret done,
> And unrecorded left through many an Age,
> Worth t' have not remained so long unsung.
>
> (I, 15–17)

Satan's temptations, in *Paradise Regained*, concern his *showing* of history to Christ. He shows actions which are memorable and worthy of being recorded, those actions which lead to fame and the nations which have become famous through their actions. *Paradise Regained*, by including history, transcends it. The usual priorities, according to Milton, are inverted as the visible is placed in the context of an unrecorded event. The conclusion is obvious: a visible history is the record of a failed temptation, as Satan knows in the council of Hell in Book I when he seeks an effective temptation. What, then, encourages its perpetuation?

The sight of history is a blinding experience. In examining Milton's understanding of Samson's career, we find that Samson's drama begins in darkness and moves (possibly) to an inner sight at the Philistine temple. Samson, as one who 'might have subdu'd the Earth, / Universally crown'd with highest praises' (174–5), thinks himself forgotten at the beginning of the play. Where he had gloried in the sight of others, he now experiences the stranger's gaze as a reproach. He is fully controlled by his situation, what others have made of him. In short, he is a man of history and stands in the play for a cultural crisis. The extreme nature of the crisis guarantees Samson's lasting fame. It is fame, however, which lives on in history while Samson is sacrificed to historical processes which feed on fame. The amazement at the end of the play is the result of Samson's transformation from a living being, weak and error prone, to a monument which will foster the continuation of history. Samson can defeat other men, but he is ultimately defeated by mankind in its ongoing concern for the *visibilia* of history. The end of *Samson Agonistes* is indeed an amazement as the 'vulgar who stood without' can go on as if nothing had happened. The crisis symbolized by Samson can be written off as a bad dream.

It is forgotten until another crisis arises which, in turn, gives birth to hallucinations and communal frenzy. What are we to make of the imaginative life of the community, perpetuated by written documents, if not that its dream life is symptomatic of disease in the body-politic? Blood-letting purges the body, but the cure is inconclusive.

In *Paradise Lost*, a sick and degenerating body is the beginning of history. History, in physical terms, is 'a Lazar-house' (XI, 479) and, as many of the allusions in this passage attest, it is the situation of the plague which has its metaphorical implications for Milton as representative of an unresolved cultural crisis. A decaying body expresses unresolved contradictions and a failure to achieve equilibrium as a result of intemperate behaviour. For Milton, Sin and Death are the ground of history and this leads to a further elaboration: history is the corpse of human endeavours. It is neither divine nor human, or, in the words of Satan in *Paradise Regained*, it is neither allegoric nor real, since history is what occurs 'in the middle'.

History is documentation through which men attempt to immortalize their achievements, their conquests, and dreams of conquest. It is what occurs 'in the middle' when men turn against each other and justify their stance in a given conflict through 'work in Wood and Stone'. The changes posited by history are not real, in the sense of different and distinguishable, because while the pictures change, the actions are the same. In *Paradise Lost*, history is a going from 'bad to worse' since every manipulation of history, every insertion of a new hero or a recent cultural transformation, dislodges the past and disrupts the present, leading to a situation of extreme instability. In other words, human history is crisis masking itself as a differentiated 'idea of progress'. But every 'progress' brings one back to history. It is a false passage and the 'bad news' of the Old Testament since its written lesson invariably comes too late and drives home the meaning of history as a finished and irrevocable past. Set out in a line, history portrays the haphazardness of human events as a crippling destiny. Put differently, history is the riddle of the Sphinx: the three ages of man when placed side by side create the sense of a monstrous reality which feeds on living bodies. Man feeds on himself, tyrannizes himself, through his proud and incestuous idols, and it is this which is not seen because to see the idols of history is to be blinded and victimized.

We have argued that until the creation of the image there is no history in heaven, and that, similarly, the making of graven images on earth introduces superstition and tyranny, the basis of history as a record of usurpations. The image is contradictory; promising unification, it leads to rivalries and contention. The purpose of histories in the Renaissance is didactic and nationalistic and its method, the construction of images which will unify a people. Yet, the images create internal strife or they lead to the discovery of an external foe, and, in this sense, become the source of further wars and misunderstanding. Christ's temptation in *Paradise Regained* involves his knowledge of history and of the roles which are available to him on the historical stage. Satan gives Christ the choice of his earthly images: he can enact his desire and imitate any of his famous predecessors, since human history is not real except as masking, posturing, and the alienating of the self in an external image. It is hallucinations which fail to acknowledge the imaginary base of all substitutions and transformations. If the processes of history are speeded up, as they are in the compression of 'parallax vision' in *Paradise Regained*, 'turning with easy eye thou mayst behold' (III, 293), its laborious oscillations converging into a single image, the '*Theban* Monster' (IV, 572).

The tyranny of the '*Theban* Monster' underlies Milton's analysis and denunciation of oracles from 'On the Morning of Christ's Nativity' to *Paradise Regained*. In the process of undergoing his own perplexing history, Milton found that the metaphors of his early poem had a literal and exact meaning. It is not, in the last resort, a question of certain privileged images, of the birth of a new, more powerful, and convincing image, but of realizing the doubleness of all images. This accounts for Milton's emerging philosophy of the iconoclast as he saw his dream of national unity and millennial glory transformed into the double monster of zealous hallucination, simply another visible history. The activity of the fallen angels, in the first two books of *Paradise Lost*, typifies this experience and shows the extent to which they have been manipulated; they deceive themselves with images. The image is ambiguous and doubling words, the sword and the plow-share of Scripture which is directed to the destruction of an old and tyrannical kingdom and promises the cultivation of a new, egalitarian society. But important in this analysis is the continuation of the active and visible might of kingdoms as recorded in histories and re-enacted by Satan in *Paradise Regained*, who still suffers the blindness of his sight. Christ, on the other hand, expresses the anti-history of revelation, a calling to individual reformation.

The literalness of *Paradise Regained* represents the demise of man as dreamed by Renaissance humanism. It stands for the death of the 'old man' and the birth of a 'greater man'; furthermore, it is a recognition that the 'old man' is the product of a particular aesthetic and historical compulsion and that the emphasis on character, as the form of history in Plutarch's *Lives* or the popular *Mirror for Magistrates*, is the source of idolatry and endless misunderstanding. This Renaissance man, expressed in Pico's 'On the Dignity of Man', is supplanted in *Paradise Regained*, not by another man or another version of man. The heroic bodies which pageant through history are not revived by Milton as history becomes, once and for all, the corpse of life. Rather, the New Testament, recorded in *Paradise Regained*, postulates the end of man. It is an 'end' in being both a revealed purpose and the closing of an age. It is not defined, however, since to do so would be to substitute a new form of aggression. The new is the undefined and the suspension of old beliefs and ways, and it is characterized by a waiting action in a space where God's ways replace images of human desire. In this respect, Milton set the stage for his mature development as early as 'On the Morning of Christ's Nativity':

> But see! the Virgin blest,
> Hath laid her Babe to rest.
>   Time is our tedious Song should here have ending;
> Heav'n's youngest-teemed Star
> Hath fixt her polisht Car,
>   Her sleeping Lord with Handmaid Lamp attending:
> And all about the Courtly Stable,
> Bright-harness'd Angels sit in order serviceable.
>
>   (Stanza XXVII)

Index